The FOUNDING *of the* UNITED STATES

1763–1815

Gerry and Janet Souter

Richard D. Brown
General Editor
Professor of History, University of Connecticut

THIS BOOK CONTAINS REMOVABLE DOCUMENTS
OF HISTORIC IMPORTANCE

METRO BOOKS
New York

METRO BOOKS
New York

An Imprint of Sterling Publishing
387 Park Avenue South
New York, NY 10016

METRO BOOKS and the distinctive Metro Books logo are
trademarks of Sterling Publishing Co., Inc.

Design © 2011, 2012 Carlton Books Ltd
Text © 2006, 2011, 2012 First Person Productions LLC

This 2012 edition published by Metro Books by
arrangement with Carlton Books Ltd.

ISBN 978-1-4351-4426-2

For information about custom editions, special sales, and
premium and corporate purchases, please contact Sterling
Special Sales at 800-805-5489 or
specialsales@sterlingpublishing.com.

Manufactured in China

2 4 6 8 10 9 7 5 3 1

www.sterlingpublishing.com

MEMORABILIA: Each facsimile document in this book carries a
code that can be found on the reverse or at the end of the document.
For example, each document in this book is coded as FOUS followed
by a series of numbers. The first number is the number of the item
and the second number refers to the pages on which information
about the document can be found.

CONTENTS

INTRODUCTION

"Freedom of men under government is to have a standing rule to live by, common to every one of that society and made by the legislative power vested in it and not to be subject to the inconstant, uncertain, arbitrary will of another man."

John Locke, 1632-1704

THE UNITED STATES OF AMERICA was wrenched from the core of the 18th Century—the "Age of Enlightenment." The journey began quietly with the scratching of a quill pen and then was thrust home at the point of a bayonet. Guttering candles at writing desks bloomed into torches leading ragged troops across frozen fields in the dead of night. The scholarly treatises of John Locke and admonitions of Jean-Jacques Rousseau were replaced with hurriedly scribbled marching orders, the simple words in soldiers' diaries, and carefully penned documents of conscience and principal.

The route to independence began in 1763 at the end of the French and Indian War. Britain was triumphant, but financially crippled and exhausted by the global Seven Years War. Their North American Colonies were a rich market for British exports and virgin ground for new taxes and duties to pay war debts. A vocal group of colonial representatives saw these taxes, these "intolerable acts" levied without colonial representation in Parliament, as grounds for separation from the mother country. A little more than a third of the colonists claimed they no longer wanted or needed Britain's so-called "protection." The line had been drawn and crossed. In April, 1775, a rattle of musketry at Lexington and Concord, Massachusetts announced the start of America's Revolutionary War.

This conflict wasn't just Americans against the British. It was also Americans against Americans. The Revolutionary War was as much a civil war as it was a battle for independence. A considerable portion of the population was loyal to the British Crown. Those Loyalists who didn't flee to Canada or Britain stayed and fought the rebels. Many of the Loyalist–Rebel battles were the most savage of the war with little quarter given.

The Revolutionary War lasted seven bloody years. With the help of France, the Americans won their independence in 1781. With that victory, the colonies had to create a new government to replace the loose collection of states joined by the wartime Articles of Confederation. They fashioned a constitution in 1787 and General George Washington, who had led the Continental Army, was elected the first President of the new independent United States of America in 1789.

In 1803, President Thomas Jefferson seized the opportunity to double the size of the country, buying 50 million acres of land from Napoleon Bonaparte. Jefferson then sent Meriwether Lewis and William Clark with their "Corps of Discovery" to explore this new Louisiana Purchase. The success of their three-year expedition drew Americans westward.

In the Mediterranean Sea, the American merchant fleet had been plundered by the Barbary Pirates of North Africa and its ships held for ransom. A handful of frigates and the United States Marines lashed back and were victorious on the shores of Tripoli. No sooner had the United States established its rights to sail the seas unmolested than they crossed swords with Britain again for pressing American sailors into the Royal Navy and confiscating "contraband" bound for France. The United States declared war in 1812. The British burned Washington and only our navy at sea and on the Great Lakes kept us from total humiliation. The Treaty of Ghent stopped the sorry affair in 1814. Our most significant victory, the Battle of New Orleans, was fought two weeks after the treaty was signed. After 52 years of striving, the United States of America had been well and truly founded.

Documenting those decades of history and gathering the images and significant memorabilia has been both humbling and uplifting. As with our other history books, we visited many of the sites, held diaries and documents written by our 18th and 19th century forbearers and stood on the ground where brave men fought and died. We shouldered flintlock muskets that once fired buck-and-ball. So many archivists, curators and scholars helped us with our work the result is a shared experience of the Founding of the United States of America.

Gerry and Janet Souter
Arlington Heights, Illinois

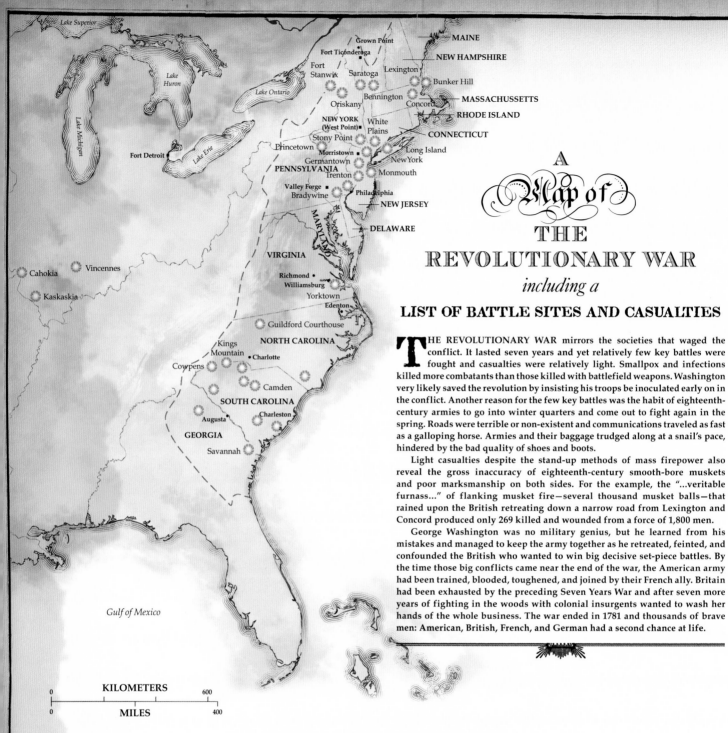

A
Map of
THE
REVOLUTIONARY WAR
including a
LIST OF BATTLE SITES AND CASUALTIES

THE REVOLUTIONARY WAR mirrors the societies that waged the conflict. It lasted seven years and yet relatively few key battles were fought and casualties were relatively light. Smallpox and infections killed more combatants than those killed with battlefield weapons. Washington very likely saved the revolution by insisting his troops be inoculated early on in the conflict. Another reason for the few key battles was the habit of eighteenth-century armies to go into winter quarters and come out to fight again in the spring. Roads were terrible or non-existent and communications traveled as fast as a galloping horse. Armies and their baggage trudged along at a snail's pace, hindered by the bad quality of shoes and boots.

Light casualties despite the stand-up methods of mass firepower also reveal the gross inaccuracy of eighteenth-century smooth-bore muskets and poor marksmanship on both sides. For the example, the "...veritable furnass..." of flanking musket fire—several thousand musket balls—that rained upon the British retreating down a narrow road from Lexington and Concord produced only 269 killed and wounded from a force of 1,800 men.

George Washington was no military genius, but he learned from his mistakes and managed to keep the army together as he retreated, feinted, and confounded the British who wanted to win big decisive set-piece battles. By the time those big conflicts came near the end of the war, the American army had been trained, blooded, toughened, and joined by their French ally. Britain had been exhausted by the preceding Seven Years War and after seven more years of fighting in the woods with colonial insurgents wanted to wash her hands of the whole business. The war ended in 1781 and thousands of brave men: American, British, French, and German had a second chance at life.

POPULATION: 3.5 million. **ENROLLED SOLDIERS:** 200,000. **PERCENTAGE:** 5.7%

TOTAL U.S. COMBAT CASUALTIES *(killed and wounded):* **10,623**
TOTAL U.S. NON-COMBAT DEATHS *(disease, accident):* **18,500**
TOTAL GERMAN *(Hessian)* COMBAT DEATHS: **1,200**
No reliable statistics for total British casualties

LEXINGTON-CONCORD	*Apr. 19, 1775*	British **269** American **90**
BUNKER/BREED'S HILL	*Jun. 17, 1775*	British **1,150** American **450**
QUEBEC	*Dec. 31, 1775*	British/Canadian **20**
		American **500**
WHITE PLAINS	*Oct. 28, 1776*	British **313** American **300**
LONG ISLAND	*Aug. 27, 1776*	British **400** American **2,000**
TRENTON	*Dec. 26, 1776*	Hessian **974** American **4**
PRINCETON	*Jan. 7, 1777*	British **98** American **41**
BRANDYWINE	*Sept. 11, 1777*	British **550** American **1,000**
FORT STANWIX	*Aug. 3, 1777*	British **150** American **150**
SARATOGA (3 battles)	*Sept. 19 – Oct 17, 1777*	British **3,500** American **500**
GERMANTOWN	*Oct. 4, 1777*	British **500** American **1,000**

MONMOUTH	*Jun. 28, 1778*	British **350** American **300**
AUGUSTA (KETTLE CREEK)	*Feb. 14, 1779*	British **140** American **32**
VINCENNES & KASKASKIA	*Feb. 23, 1779*	British **2** American **0**
SAVANNAH	*Oct. 9, 1779*	British **57** American/French **800**
CHARLESTOWN	*May 12, 1780*	British **0** American **8**
CAMDEN	*Aug. 16, 1780*	British **324** American **1,000**
KINGS MOUNTAIN	*Oct. 7, 1780*	Tories **300** American **90**
COWPENS	*Jan. 17, 1781*	British **100** (829 captured)
		American **72**
GUILFORD COURTHOUSE	*Mar. 15, 1781*	British **500** American **250**
YORKTOWN	*Sept. 28 - Oct 19, 1781*	British **500** American **80**
		French **200**

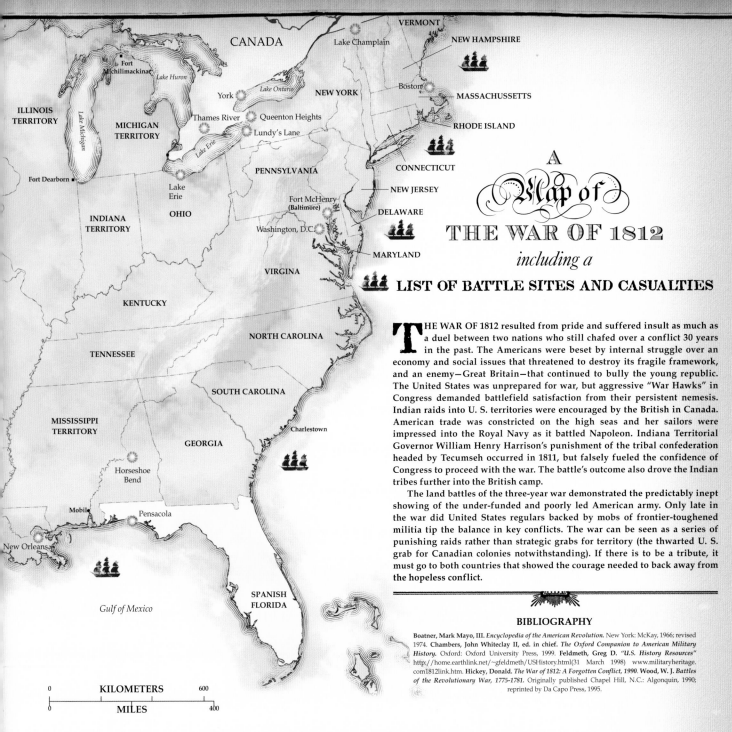

A Map of
THE WAR OF 1812
including a
LIST OF BATTLE SITES AND CASUALTIES

THE WAR OF 1812 resulted from pride and suffered insult as much as a duel between two nations who still chafed over a conflict 30 years in the past. The Americans were beset by internal struggle over an economy and social issues that threatened to destroy its fragile framework, and an enemy—Great Britain—that continued to bully the young republic. The United States was unprepared for war, but aggressive "War Hawks" in Congress demanded battlefield satisfaction from their persistent nemesis. Indian raids into U. S. territories were encouraged by the British in Canada. American trade was constricted on the high seas and her sailors were impressed into the Royal Navy as it battled Napoleon. Indiana Territorial Governor William Henry Harrison's punishment of the tribal confederation headed by Tecumseh occurred in 1811, but falsely fueled the confidence of Congress to proceed with the war. The battle's outcome also drove the Indian tribes further into the British camp.

The land battles of the three-year war demonstrated the predictably inept showing of the under-funded and poorly led American army. Only late in the war did United States regulars backed by mobs of frontier-toughened militia tip the balance in key conflicts. The war can be seen as a series of punishing raids rather than strategic grabs for territory (the thwarted U. S. grab for Canadian colonies notwithstanding). If there is to be a tribute, it must go to both countries that showed the courage needed to back away from the hopeless conflict.

BIBLIOGRAPHY

Boatner, Mark Mayo, III. *Encyclopedia of the American Revolution.* New York: McKay, 1966; revised 1974. Chambers, John Whiteclay II, ed. in chief. *The Oxford Companion to American Military History.* Oxford: Oxford University Press, 1999. Feldmeth, Greg D. *"U.S. History Resources"* http://home.earthlink.net/~gfeldmeth/USHistory.html(31 March 1998) www.militaryheritage.com1812link.htm. Hickey, Donald. *The War of 1812: A Forgotten Conflict, 1990.* Wood, W. J. *Battles of the Revolutionary War, 1775-1781.* Originally published Chapel Hill, N.C.: Algonquin, 1990; reprinted by Da Capo Press, 1995.

U. S. POPULATION: 7.6 million. **ENROLLED SOLDIERS:** 286,000. **PERCENTAGE:** 3.8%

TOTAL U.S. CASUALTIES *(and wounded)*: **6,765**
TOTAL BRITISH CASUALTIES *(killed and wounded)*: **5,000**

Battle	Date	Casualties	Battle	Date	Casualties
TIPPICANOE	*Nov. 7, 1811*	Tecumseh Confederacy **120** Militia **188**	LUNDY'S LANE	*Jul. 25, 1814*	British **1,000+** American **1,300**
MICHILIMACKINAC (FORT MACKINAC)	*Jul. 17, 1812*	British **0** American **60**	WASHINGTON, DC	*Aug. 24, 1814*	British **249** American **50**
FORT DETROIT	*Aug. 8, 1812*	British/Indian **?** American **2,200**	LAKE CHAMPLAIN (PLATTSBURGH)	*Sept. 6-11, 1814*	British **300** American **200**
FORT DEARBORN	*Aug. 15, 1812*	Indian **?** American **80 of 93**	BALTIMORE (FT. MCHENRY)	*Sept. 12-14, 1814*	British **346** American **310**
QUEENSTON HEIGHTS	*Oct. 13, 1812*	British **119** American **900**	PENSACOLA, FLA	*Nov. 7-9, 1814*	British/Spanish **(negligible)** American **15**
YORK	*Apr. 22, 1813*	British **440** American **320**	NEW ORLEANS	*Jan. 8, 1815*	British **2,036** American **71**
LAKE ERIE	*Sept. 10, 1813*	British **135** American **123**			
THAMES RIVER	*Oct. 5, 1813*	British **188** American **45**			
HORSESHOE BEND	*Mar. 27, 1814*	Creek/Red Stick Indians **800** American Militia **203**			

THE FRENCH & INDIAN WAR ENDS—1763

By 1761, most of the shooting in the French and Indian War had stopped and Great Britain held dominion over virtually all of what had once belonged to France on the continent of North America. In 1759, General James Wolfe had died on the Plains of Abraham before the fall of Quebec. In 1755, General Edward Braddock had been cut down by Ojibwa and Pottawatomie Indians near the banks of Pennsylvania's Monongahela River. Rank upon rank of Britain's Redcoat infantry had suffered ambush and—worse—capture by the tribes allied with France. Britain had paid in blood for its new empire.

Settlers yanked arrows from their doors; charred log walls were replaced by green lumber; the dead were buried; and colonial militias snaked along forest paths toward farms, shops, and home. Back they went to business as usual as hard-working and loyal subjects of the British Crown. But business, they discovered on their return, was anything but "usual."

ABOVE *The death of British General James Wolfe on the Plains of Abraham during the siege of Quebec in 1759. Eventually, the British captured Quebec from the French.*

Britain's North American colonies had enjoyed considerable prosperity under the Crown: guaranteed markets for their crops; protection from French, Spanish, and Dutch piracy at sea; and the rule of British law. On the other hand, the balance of trade had been one-sided; more products were imported from the Mother Country than exported there and British investors inclined toward exploitation of their colonial subjects. However, a mutually agreeable peace had been forged. The signing of the Treaty of Paris in 1763 formalized the new Pax Britannica map of North America. In the same year, fearing problems with the Indian tribes and the westward explorations of the colonials, King George III forbade his "loving subjects" from exploring or trading beyond the Appalachian Mountains. Chief Pontiac, head of the Council of Three Tribes (the Ottawa, Pottawatomie, and Ojibwa), was angered over this downturn in their fortunes and began destroying British forts. Citing this savagery, Britain sent 10,000 troops to Boston "for the protection of the colonies." This force represented the first step by the British Parliament toward dealing with the Indians and establishing garrisons to enforce the success of future revenue schemes. The colonists would now pay the piper.

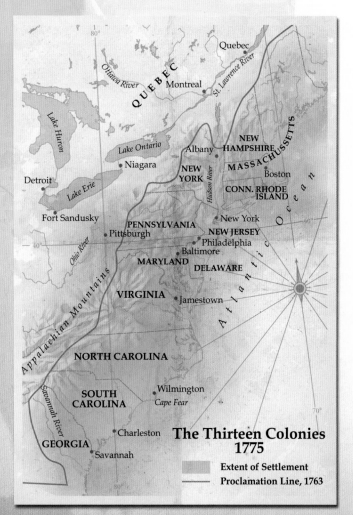

The Thirteen Colonies 1775

Extent of Settlement
Proclamation Line, 1763

LEFT *The original 13 colonies following the French and Indian War and the "Proclamation line" drawn by the British beyond which the colonists could not settle. Many ignored the line.*

In truth, the British Exchequer was broke. The small nation shouldered a debt of £140 million and the British were heavily taxed just to pay the interest. Parliament began developing ideas focused on the colonies to generate revenue.

This sea change in Great Britain's attitude was not lost on the 13 colonies. Agitators stood up at public meetings or published pamphlets expounding "treasonous" ideas. Crown governors, magistrates, and tax collectors began writing nervous letters back home. Even Southern planters, the profits from whose tobacco crops were cherished by the Mother Country, joined the debate. One colonel of the Virginia militia, who had married into the upper strata of the planter aristocracy, showed growing concern. George Washington was a man of considerable stature in his community both physically—at six foot two inches tall—and as a leader in the field. His leadership had been tested in the war and inexperience had caused him a humiliating surrender. But later as a volunteer aide-de-camp to General Braddock, he led British survivors from the Monongahela River ambush, and at age 31 he returned to Virginia a war hero. His guidance would continue to be called upon in the Virginia legislature.

Over the next 14 years, the triumph over France, won side-by-side with their British cousins, diminished and soured for the colonists. Setting aside deep-rooted parochial differences, Massachusetts men sat with Virginians, and Rhode Islanders conversed openly with South Carolinians. They met in taverns and churches totting up their grievances and many began to think of themselves less as subjects of the Crown and more as "Americans."

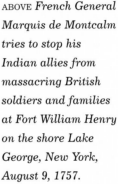

ABOVE *French General Marquis de Montcalm tries to stop his Indian allies from massacring British soldiers and families at Fort William Henry on the shore Lake George, New York, August 9, 1757.*

ABOVE RIGHT *General George Washington: oil on canvas painting by Rembrandt Peale in a gold frame. Washington wore this uniform of his own design throughout the French and Indian War.*

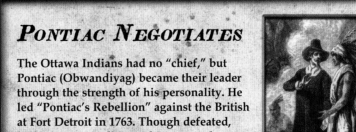

THE INTOLERABLE ACTS
1764–1768

The Seven Years' War (1756–63) and the French and Indian War had achieved the desired end for Britain— expansion of its empire at the expense of France and Spain. A generation of Europeans had been slaughtered on the battlefield. To meet their debts, the British government now needed to wring revenue from all their subjects. From a casual state of "salutary neglect," the North American Colonies had to be brought to heel, or at least closer to parity in taxation with the British in the Mother Country.

In 1764, George Grenville, Britain's Chancellor of the Exchequer, pushed through the American Revenue Act—also called the Sugar Act. It reduced the tax on foreign molasses coming into the colonies. However, it also added new taxes on refined sugar, coffee, Spanish wine, and non-British textiles. In addition, a vice-admiralty court was established in Halifax, Nova Scotia, with jurisdiction over most of North America. The principle of trial by one's peers was threatened. Grenville's measures also included a Currency Act that forbade the printing of money by the colonies, and so, by devaluing colonial paper, favored British creditors over colonial debtors.

ABOVE *This cartoon originally appeared in Benjamin Franklin's* Gazette *in 1754. It suggested that only by joining together would the united colonies survive.*

ABOVE *Stamps issued under the 1765 Stamp Act. Those who paid the tax on their newspaper or legal documents received an offical stamp, raising £60,000 a year to pay the crown's war debt. The impostion of the tax inflamed the colonies more than the cost.*

The imposition of new taxes eventually caused some of the merchants in Boston, New York, Philadelphia, and Charleston to create non-importation agreements that halted new orders of many British luxury goods. But the decree that brought all the colonists—including the Friends of Government—to their feet was the Stamp Act of 1765.

This tax—named for the stamp which the act required be affixed to items taxed under its regulations—extended to newspapers, legal documents, business papers, almanacs, pamphlets, and even playing cards and dice. And it had to be paid in hard-to-find gold or silver British pounds sterling. By adding an estimated £60,000 in revenue from this act to the £45,000 gathered by the Sugar Act, the Crown expected to raise about one-third of the money needed to maintain troops and an army of civil servants in the American colonies. This all made perfect sense to Parliament, but a great hue and cry arose

TARRING AND FEATHERING TAX COLLECTORS

Tarring and feathering became a uniquely American method of intimidating undesirable persons and making a statement against unwanted laws. Hot tar swabbed on the bare skin raised painful blisters. Feathers were added for further humiliating effect. Removal of the tar pulled out hairs, and turpentine used to soften the tar seared the blisters. Crown tax collectors became the chief targets. Passage of the Townshend Acts and the Tea Act resulted in the death of several tax collectors and Tory (British Loyalist) sympathizers.

that filled colonial pamphlets and newspapers. Gangs of young toughs were organized, calling themselves the Sons of Liberty. Violence became rampant against government appointees, stamp-masters, and tax-collectors in Boston and New York.

To create a united opposition front, the province of Massachusetts proposed a Stamp Act Congress. Twenty-six delegates from nine of the 13 colonies showed up in New York. The Royal Governors of Virginia, Georgia, and North Carolina refused to allow the election of delegates. New Hampshire declined the invitation.

As royal tax-collectors resigned their commissions and packed their bags, the overwhelming non-importation opposition led English merchants to argue for the repeal of the Stamp Act. However, Great Britain asserted its right to tax when and where it wished and pressed the argument that the colonies were "virtually represented" in Parliament just as well as some English Boroughs that did not elect members. This obdurate stance was reinforced by the Townshend Acts. Levies were made on glass, paint, paper, lead, and tea. Once again, taxation without representation was the colonial battle cry. This time, however, many American towns not only drew up non-importation agreements, but also began encouraging local manufacturing of specified goods. Self-sufficiency was another step toward self-government.

Finally, in 1768, as vandalism and violence accelerated in the coastal towns, two regiments of British Regulars were shipped to Boston. Most previous detachments of troops that had landed had been marched inland to frontier forts, but these 4,000 regulars remained in the city as a garrison force. While loyal Friends of Government nodded approval, other men of means, intellect, and action drew together to discuss the path to treason.

BELOW *Marinus Willet, French-Indian war veteran, prevents the confiscation of firearms by the British on June 6, 1775. The British army came to be seen as an occupying force as rebellion spread throughout the colonies.*

BELOW *Patrick Henry achieved fame as a politician and orator. Shown here in a Virginia court-house in 1763, his famous appeal "Give me liberty or give me death" was passionately proclaimed in 1775.*

BRITISH SEVEN YEARS' WAR DEBT

Curiously, before 1763, American colonials paid the lowest taxes of any citizens in the western world. Colonial subjects were taxed about one shilling per head per year. In Great Britain, subjects faced taxes of 26 shillings each. A series of wars that began in 1688 were responsible for Great Britain's enormous debt. Between 1756 and 1763 alone, the British national debt doubled to £150 million. This burden required £4 million each year in interest alone. Ordinary Britons staged riots to let Parliament know they would accept no more tax increases.

REBELS & REDCOATS COLLIDE
1770–1774

In Boston, the year 1770 started out beneath a veneer of calm, in contrast to the five turbulent years that had preceded it. Couriers raced from town to village carrying sheaves of the latest patriot broadsides and newspapers. Behind closed doors, the colonists debated whether to stay loyal to the Crown, to join the Rebels, or to stay neutral. And in the light of day, to the relief of those "Friends of Government" who would become "Loyalists," red-coated British soldiers strolled in pairs or marched in squads.

British soldiers were poorly paid and were forced to look for odd jobs in Boston to earn extra money. The city's local toughs and idlers had marked these "King's men" and insulted the job-seeking soldiers, driving them from employers' doors. Soon, bitter soldiers and local agitators roamed the streets seeking each other out. On the cold night of March 5, 1770, jeering Bostonians armed with snowballs set upon a squad of harried and nervous soldiers on King Street. The taunts became slanderous. The crowd pressed closer around the squad. A flint snapped down into its powder pan and a booming shot echoed off the street stonework. A ragged clatter of shots followed and a cloud of powder smoke drifted over five civilian bodies on the cobblestones.

The effects of the event were inflamed by rhetoric from political protester Samuel Adams. Silversmith and rebel propagandist Paul Revere ran off an engraving depicting the event as a brutal slaying of innocent bystanders—the image was circulated on broadsides throughout the colonies. The soldiers were tried in a civilian court and defended by three colonial lawyers including Samuel Adams'

ABOVE *A sketch drawn by Paul Revere based on eyewitness reports of the so-called Boston Massacre. It is an inaccurate depiction, but fueled the rebels' need for action against such British "atrocities."*

cousin, John Adams. Of the nine British soldiers tried, seven were set free, but the "Boston Massacre," as the incident became known, had been etched into the public consciousness.

Two years later, a challenge emerged to the fine old Rhode Island traditions of freedom of the sea, blockade-running, and smuggling. The armed schooner *Gaspee*, commanded by Crown revenue collector, Lieutenant William Duddingston, became a symbol of the arrogance of British oppression. In Duddingston's eyes all small boat-owners plying the Rhode Island coast were guilty of something. He regularly chased them down, often fired cannon shot across their bows, boarded them, and found reasons to levy fines. The governor of Rhode Island, Joseph Wanton, complained to Admiral Montagu, the commander of the British fleet, yet received nothing but contempt in return.

On June 9, 1772, Captain Benjamin Lindsey set sail from the harbor of Newport in the packet sloop *Hannah* on a

PAUL REVERE
PROPAGANDIST

Paul Revere (1735–1818) learned silversmithing from his father and served as a lieutenant in the army in 1755. He became the premier silver and coppersmith in Boston, but as tensions grew with the British, he joined the Sons of Liberty and the Committees of Correspondence, serving as a frequent messenger on horseback. His political cartoons, engraved in copper for printing, were powerful tools to inflame public opinion. Revere's version of the "Boston Massacre"—though largely inaccurate—became a powerful piece of anti-British propaganda.

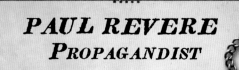

DOCUMENT:

1. This page introduces the Quartering Act of 1774, which allowed British officers to quarter their troops in private homes or outbuildings if no barracks were available. This measure continued the Quartering Act of 1765. See envelope, page 19.

See envelope, page 19.

AMERICAN PRIVATEERS

Before Americans had a navy, the Continental Congress had to rely on issuing "letters of marque"—literally licenses to private ship owners to arm their vessels and capture British merchant ships. The colonists licensed 1,697 privateers, sending almost 15,000 guns to sea, and capturing more than 2,000 British ships and their valuable cargos. New England, Maine, and Rhode Island had considerable experience with smuggling by the time the Revolution started and put their law-evading seamanship in the service of their country.

LEFT *The* Gaspee *was a British revenue schooner that pursued colonial smugglers. When it ran aground, Rhode Island colonists captured the crew and set it afire on June 9, 1772.*

course to Providence, Rhode Island. The *Gaspee* appeared astern and sent a ball from her chaser across Lindsey's bow. The packet swept inshore to round Namquid Point. Duddingston tried to cut off the close-hauled packet. Except for a shoal, he would have made it. The *Gaspee* struck hard and buried her keel in the sand. Lindsey arrived in Providence at 5.00 p.m. at the house of his friend John Brown, and a call was put out to gather seafaring Rhode Islanders together for an evening's outing. To the rattling tattoo of a drum, a large party of armed men arrived. They shared a glass or two while lead was melted and molded into fresh shot for their muskets and blunderbusses. Captain Abraham Whipple led the boats, their oarlocks muffled, from Fenner's Wharf into the dark. A short time later there was a distant rattle of gunfire, and then the night was lit up by a glow of flames. The boats returned and the *Gaspee* was no more. Admiral Montagu complained to Governor Wanton, but, apparently, no one ashore had seen anything. Whitehall created a Royal Commission to investigate and prosecute, but no arrests were ever made.

BELOW *The "Sons of Liberty" pull down an equestrian statue of George III, as respectable New Yorkers look on. The statue's head was mounted outside a pub and the rest melted down into lead balls for colonial muskets.*

BELOW LEFT *The tricorn, or three-cornered, hat was popular headgear for much of the eighteenth century, but was generally out of fashion in Europe by the time the French Revolution began in 1789. They were made of pressed felt and expensive in the American Colonies.*

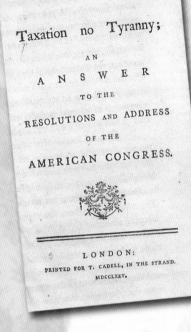

Taxation no Tyranny;

AN

ANSWER

TO THE

RESOLUTIONS AND ADDRESS

OF THE

AMERICAN CONGRESS.

LONDON:
PRINTED FOR T. CADELL, IN THE STRAND.
MDCCLXXV.

ABOVE *British Prime Minister, Lord Frederick North, had this pamphlet printed in 1775 to counter the colonies' claim of "taxation without representation." North reaffirmed Britain's right to tax and levy as it saw fit.*

In the early 1770s, 17 million pounds of tea sat in warehouses owned by the East India Company, which was struggling financially. To keep the venerable old firm from going under, London lawmakers passed the Tea Act in 1773, which specified that this surplus tea be sent only to approved Crown agents in the colonies. It seemed to signal the first of many possible monopolies that might be foisted on colonial merchants by the Crown. For colonists to drink this tainted tea would be a disloyal act against free trade. So, up and down the North American coast, crates of tea splashed into the Atlantic Ocean.

In Boston, that hotbed of radicals, rebellion was transformed into a theatrical production on the night of December 16, 1773. Goaded on by Samuel Adams and merchant John Hancock, a mob of 150 locals, their faces daubed with cork and with feathers in their hair, boarded the tea ships at Griffin's Wharf disguised as "Mohawk Indians," and threw 342 cases of tea worth £9,000 overboard into Boston Harbor. When word reached London in January 1774, Prime Minister Frederick, Lord North, was not amused. He rounded on the colonies with five Coercive Acts designed to put the colonies—and especially Massachusetts—in their place.

The port of Boston was closed until the cost of the spoiled tea was repaid. Massachusetts was virtually placed under direct Crown rule as its charter of 1691 was revoked and town meetings prohibited. The Quartering Act of 1765 was extended to stationing troops in "quarters other than barracks," such as people's homes. Also, if any British official were to be charged with a capital crime, he would be tried in Britain where he could find an acquittal-minded jury. The final straw was the Quebec Act—not part of the "Coercive Acts" but passed at the same time.

> *"Let freemen be represented by numbers alone. The distinctions between Virginians, Pennsylvanians, New Yorkers, New Englanders are no more. I am not a Virginian, but an American!"*
>
> **PATRICK HENRY**
> **FIRST CONTINENTAL CONGRESS, 1774**

GEORGE WASHINGTON
PLANTER & SLAVE OWNER

In 1743 when George Washington was 11 years old, he inherited 10 slaves and 500 acres of land on the death of his father. By the time he was 22, that number had grown to 36, and to this were added 20 slaves by his marriage to Martha Custis in 1759. As the Washingtons' home at Mount Vernon grew, so did the number of men, women, and families needed to operate the plantation. By 1799, when Washington died, 316 slaves lived on his estate.

TEA
THE DRINK OF CHOICE

The American colonists brought their tea drinking habits with them from the Mother Country. Until they were transplanted to the North American shores, how the tea reached them was of no consequence. Since the Dutch had opened the tea trade in 1610, the British-controlled East India Company had a monopoly on English tea trade from China. Tea's caffeine was a pick-me-up and boiling the water to drink it killed bacteria. After the Boston Tea Party, however, many Americans became patriotic coffee drinkers.

BELOW *This group of children has attached a paper sign reading "Tory" to the back of a dignified gentleman. As war drew closer, friends of the British Crown were increasingly harassed by patriots.*

This granted financial relief and religious freedom to Roman Catholics in addition to expanding the Canadian border southward to the rich Ohio Valley—land long coveted by Virginia. That slap in the face brought George Mason, Peyton Randolph, Richard Henry Lee, and George Washington into the New England radical camp.

With the Coercive Acts rolling off colonial presses in May 1774, dozen of riders, including Paul Revere, saddled up and pounded through the countryside as far south as Philadelphia, warning of Boston's impending blockade and Britain's noxious punishments. Many colonies began to send aid—money, rice, meat on the hoof, and other goods—to the besieged city. Anti-loyalist leaders, who were already outraged, joined together to issue invitations to the colonies to send representatives to what became the First Continental Congress. Fifty-six delegates from 12 colonies—Georgia did not participate—gathered at Philadelphia's Carpenter's Hall on September 5, 1774. Many of the attendees had never previously strayed beyond the borders of their home colonies.

The delegates began by establishing a one colony–one vote procedure that lasted through Continental Congress deliberations until 1789. Their foresight also determined that Peyton Randolph of Virginia be elected the first president of Congress. This move further wedded the wealthy and populous Virginians to the rebel cause. As the delegates began their work, Paul Revere reined in long enough to drop off a copy of the "Suffolk Resolves," a collection penned by angry Massachusetts men of Suffolk County that included every possible renunciation of British Acts and edicts going back 10 years. The reading of the Resolves brought forth a hurrah and a rush to send it unchanged to London. Conservative delegates softened the final document that was shipped to Parliament, but 56 colonists had stood together in congress and sent an irreversible message of defiance.

THE DESTRUCTION OF TEA AT BOSTON HARBOR.

LEFT *Dressed as Mohawk Indians, a group of the Sons of Liberty boarded an English ship and dumped 342 chests of tea into Boston Harbor—a protest against the tea tax.*

15

GUNFIRE AT LEXINGTON & CONCORD—1775

On the night of April 18, 1775, Paul Revere was awakened and told that two lanterns burned in the steeple of Boston's Old North Church. This message signaled that British troops were being rowed to Cambridge for a raid on Lexington to capture Samuel Adams and John Hancock, and then on to Concord to seize rebel stores of gunpowder, supplies, and four brass cannon. Revere was taken to a boat and rowed to the Cambridge shore where a saddled horse awaited him. He arrived in Lexington at the parsonage of Reverend Jonas Clarke where Adams and Hancock were staying. A local man acting as a makeshift sentry complained about his shouting. Revere reportedly exclaimed, "Noise! You'll have more noise than this before long. The regulars are coming out!"

William Dawes Jr., a patriot radical from an old Boston family, joined Revere on the road at about 12:30 a.m. and they continued on to Concord. Dr. Samuel Prescott, who had been visiting a friend in Lexington, soon accompanied them in their gallop. All three were suddenly stopped by a British patrol, one of many sent ahead for just that purpose by General Thomas Gage, commander-in-chief of the British army in America. Prescott spurred clear of the trap and Dawes managed to escape a bit later, but Revere was dismounted and held. However, now the word was out, and church bells began tolling on down the road.

Following the three dusty patriots came rank on rank of Britain's best, a picked force of 700 grenadiers and light infantry commanded by Lieutenant Colonel Francis Smith of the 10th Lincolnshires and Major John Pitcairn of the Royal Marines. The soldiers had been

> " We must fight!
> Is life so dear, or peace so sweet as to be purchased at the price of chains and slavery? Forbid it, almighty God! I know not what course others may take, but as for me, give me liberty or give me death!"
>
> PATRICK HENRY,
> VIRGINIA LEGISLATURE

GENERAL THOMAS GAGE

Thomas Gage (1720–1787) was a British general and became governor of Massachusetts in 1774, after Parliament passed the Coercive Acts in retaliation for the 1773 Boston Tea Party. He had fought during the Seven Years' War, and with General Braddock at Montreal. In 1763, he became commander-in-chief of British Forces in North America. On April 17, 1775, Gage was ordered by Parliament to take "vigorous action" against the American rebels. The Lexington–Concord debacle on April 19 eventually forced his removal from command.

BELOW *This map shows the route from Lexington and Concord that was followed by the British troops. Revere and his companions also followed this route.*

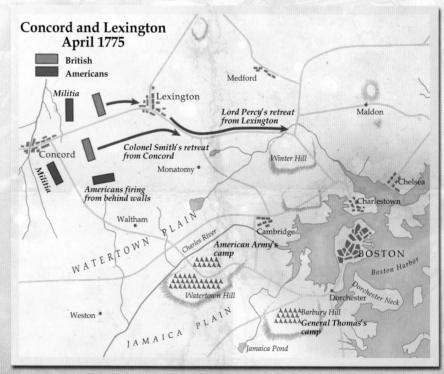

Concord and Lexington April 1775

British
Americans

Militia

Lexington

Medford

Maldon

Lord Percy's retreat from Lexington

Concord

Militia

Colonel Smith's retreat from Concord

Monatomy

Winter Hill

Chelsea

Americans firing from behind walls

Charlestown

Waltham

WATERTOWN PLAIN

Charles River

Cambridge

American Army's camp

BOSTON

Boston Harbor

Watertown Hill

Dorchester

Dorchester Neck

Weston

JAMAICA PLAIN

Barbury Hill

General Thomas's camp

Jamaica Pond

RIGHT *This contemporary engraving from a watercolor by Amos Doolittle is a crude but accurate depiction of the brief, one-sided battle fought at Lexington between farmers, shopkeepers, and the British Regulars.*

BELOW *Amos Doolittle's painting follows the Redcoats' march through Concord along a road that will be flanked by rebel fire. Major John Pitcairn and Lieutenant Colonel Francis Smith reconnoiter from a hilltop.*

"THE REGULARS ARE OUT" HIDE YOUR CANNON!

On April 18, 1775, Dr. Joseph Warren asked Paul Revere to ride to Lexington and warn Samuel Adams and John Hancock that British soldiers were coming for them, and that they then planned to march on to Concorde to capture hidden military stores, including four brass cannon. Two of those brasscannon were named the "Hancock" and "Adams." They were used throughout the war, and the "Adams" is at the Bunker Hill memorial today.

roused from their beds after final tattoo, packed into rowboats like sardines, and had slogged through knee-deep water before the long dusty march. These were men in a foul mood. As they marched, figures could be glimpsed, running on unseen trails through the dense, dark woods.

On Lexington Green, Captain John Parker, commander of two companies of 100 local militia—the Minute Men and the Alarm Men—stood with his neighbors dressed in homespun garb, armed with hunting rifles and fowling pieces. In the gray damp of dawn, Major Pitcairn arrived and wheeled the British infantry ranks into line. Shoemaker Sylvanus Wood remembered, "There they halted. The officer then swung his sword and said, 'Lay down your arms you damned rebels, or you are all dead men!'"

A shot rang out, followed by a high, ragged volley from the regulars. Parker dispersed his men. As they took cover, a second killing volley cut into them. British troops continued their march to Concord past the bodies of eight dead militiamen.

At Concord, the British were met by a larger body of men and fifes and drums across the green of the Muster Field. Volleys of ball and shot licked out. Gusts of gun smoke washed over the village as the militia's ranks swelled from nearby villages and the British retreated. The road back toward Lexington became, as Minute Man Amos Barrett recalled " … a veritable furnass of musquetry."

That furnace of fire never slackened as frustrated British soldiers burned and plundered homes along the road. The exhausted expedition was relieved at Lexington by a force of over 1,000 troops from the Boston garrison. And still the gunfire continued. In the wake of the retreat, powder-blackened shopkeepers, herdsmen, shoemakers, and farmers leaned on their still-warm weapons. A long, bloody war had just begun.

BREED'S HILL & BUNKER HILL 1775

ABOVE *The right flank of the British line advances to the sound of drums, muskets at the ready, eyes front. Ineffective artillery support doomed their early attacks and wasted these brave men.*

DR. JOSEPH WARREN

Dr. Warren (1741–1775) was a prominent Boston patriot influenced by Samuel Adams and active in the early struggle against British taxes and edicts. He became a doctor after graduating from Harvard. To oppose the Townshend Acts he wrote scathing articles under the nom de plume "True Patriot." His chairmanship of the Boston Committee of Safety led to a commission as major general in the Massachusetts militia. He was killed by a musket ball in the defense of Breed's Hill.

Once again, young men on fast horses fanned out from Boston. They carried the word about the "victory" at Lexington and Concord. The King's troops had been fired upon. Newspapers printed the casualty lists of dead and wounded patriots.

Major Generals William Howe, Henry Clinton, and John Burgoyne arrived in Boston on May 25, 1775, to find 6,000 British troops bottled up by a motley collection of untrained bumpkins. The new arrivals implored General Gage to secure the Dorchester Heights above Charlestown, thereby dominating Boston and providing an attack base against the rebels gathering to the south. By June 13, the entire British plan was in rebel hands, and after much debate Artemas Ward, the militia's general, was charged by the Committee of Safety with the defense of Dorchester Heights.

On June 16, Colonel William Prescott paraded his command of 1,200 men from Massachusetts and Connecticut, plus an "artillery train" of two four-pounder cannon that rattled over the cobbles. His "army" was a mob of civilians poked into ranks, who carried a collection of odd arms, from 20-year-old muskets to shotguns, blunderbusses, and Spanish fusees. After debate en route, Breed's Hill overlooking Boston was chosen as the primary fortification, with Bunker Hill above Charlestown Neck as the backup. Prescott's diggers arrived atop Breed's at dead of night and began to build a redoubt of fire-step trenches, hogshead barrels filled with dirt, and bundles of wood-branch fascines completing a square with sides 132 feet long.

At dawn on June 17, General Howe was amazed to discover the fortress that had sprung up overnight on the heights. He and his colleagues noted; "Never give the Yankees time to dig." Howe's sound plan of a frontal attack and flank envelopment of Breed's Hill was delayed by six hours until his 1,500 infantry and 12 guns were in position. The beginning of the battle came with a few rounds fired from the British frigate *Lively*. Those shots awoke Brigadier General Israel Putnam who galloped off to the hills. "Old Put" raided Prescott's diggers to improve the fortification of Bunker Hill. Grimy and game, the remaining 500 men settled in to await the British. Prescott and his officers, including Major John Stark and Captain Thomas Knowlton, had learned their trade in the French and Indian War. All their skills would be needed.

After a bombardment by the *Lively*, *Falcon*, and the 64-gun ship of the line *Somerset*, the British attack developed. Prepared to sweep aside untutored militia, the attacking troops were surprised by the organized defense. Stark's men at the landing beach ripped through the light infantry with disciplined volley fire by rank. "Fire at the top of their gaiters or the waistcoat!" Stark shouted. Struggling under 50 pounds of marching rations, ammunition, and accoutrements, the British clambered up the hills into scything fire. To the rebels' rear, Charlestown had been set afire by British heated shot and exploding shot. General Ward desperately tried to gather reinforcements, while Putnam galloped from hill to hill.

Grenadiers facing up the slope toward Knowlton's fence line blazed out a platoon volley that tore though the air above the militiamen. The answering volley, aimed low, sent grenadiers tumbling, their black bearskins bouncing down the hill. At 60 yards, 30 yards, 20 yards, militia volleys decimated the British front ranks. But numbers, discipline, and clouds of grapeshot foretold the end as, after three attacks, Howe and Clinton had secured both hills by the end of the day. The butcher's bill for the 2,500 British troops was 45 percent casualties. The Americans suffered 441 casualties out of their 1,500 engaged. The bumpkins had showed they had the makings of an army.

Brigadier General Israel "Old Put" Putnam galloped back and forth between Breed's and Bunker Hill, sword in hand, rallying the farmers, militia, and shopkeepers to keep firing.

ABOVE *This engraving shows the last moments of the rear guard atop Breed's Hill as the British arrived. The farmers and shopkeepers held out against the bayonet as their fellow patriots successfully retreated.*

TOP *The defenders of Breed's Hill used a variety of flintlock weapons like this short-barreled coach gun loaded with buckshot, old Spanish Fusees, fowling pieces, trade muskets and hunting rifles.*

ABOVE *This painting by Trumbull captures the grim attack on Breed's Hill. British Regulars lean into the slope of the hill as the torrent of lead shot pours into their ranks.*

ARTILLERY FAILURE AT BREED'S HILL

Had the British been able to properly deploy their artillery at Breed's Hill, the outcome might have been different. To bombard the redoubt at the crest, ships' guns were first employed, but the 9–12 pound cannon could not be properly elevated and the target was beyond the 1,200-yard accuracy range of these weapons. Howe's artillery became mired in the marshy ground and then it was discovered the six-pounders had been provided with 12-pound shot. After horrific casualties, grape shot was finally used to carry the American redoubt.

WASHINGTON CHOSEN TO LEAD
1776

RIGHT *The Grand Union was the flag of an American army that still had no name when they bottled up the British in Boston. During the Revolution, the army fought under many "American" flags.*

LEFT *Washington had only commanded militia when Congress picked him to lead the army. He looked like a general and he dressed like one. His men readily accepted him as their leader.*

The militia's adventure atop Breed's and Bunker Hills ended in retreat, but the rag-tag band led by experienced officers had dealt the British a drubbing and then withdrawn in good order. This action seemed to justify a request made by the Massachusetts Committee of Safety before the battle. The committee had penned a letter to the Second Continental Congress sitting in the Pennsylvania State House asking that their militia be adopted as an "American Army" for all the colonies. But who could lead such a force?

On June 14, John Adams rose to nominate "a gentleman whose skill as an officer, whose independent fortune, great talents and universal character would command the respect of America and unite the full exertions of the colonies better than any other person alive, a gentleman of Virginia who is among us here and well known to all of us."

As Colonel Prescott led his men toward Breed's Hill on June 16, 1775, the president of Congress, John Hancock, offered the leadership of the Continental Army to the Virginia militia colonel, George Washington. On accepting, the 43-year-old Washington read a prepared statement expressing doubt in his own abilities, but pledging that he would do his best; "As to pay, Sir, I beg leave to Assure the Congress that no pecuniary consideration could have tempted me to have accepted this Arduous employment … I do not wish to make any proffit from it."

Barely more than two weeks later, on a rainy Sunday, July 2, 1775, General Washington rode into Cambridge to inspect his command. At his side was Major General Charles Lee, an ambitious ex-British officer. Washington traveled to each militia encampment, and as he did so men stood by their campfires and quietly doffed their wide-brimmed and tricorn hats. Officers gathered to him: Artemas Ward of Massachusetts; John Glover and his fishermen from Marblehead; the well turned-out Rhode Islanders with their young commander, 33-year-old Nathanael Greene. There was even a portly, 25-year-old, bespectacled bookseller, Henry Knox, who seemed to have a bookworm's encyclopedic knowledge of artillery.

HENRY KNOX

Born to a poor family, Henry Knox (1750–1806) quit school to apprentice as a bookbinder when his father abandoned the family. He opened his own bookstore at age 21 and began reading books on war and strategy. The rotund youth with glasses and a knowledge of guns and defenses caught Washington's attention while inspecting the militia. Soon, Knox rose to be chief of artillery. His command of guns and personal courage throughout the war eventually earned him the post of Washington's Secretary of War.

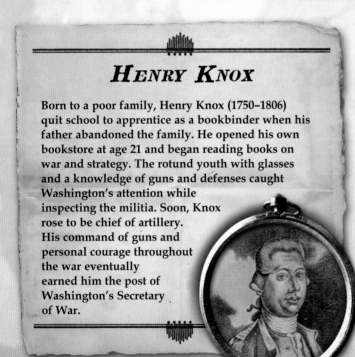

BELOW *Henry Knox's "noble train of artillery" and its transport over 300 miles through snow and over frozen rivers from Fort Ticonderoga to Boston was an outstanding feat of arms.*

Washington passed the summer in shaping up his blockading army. The British made only small raids and lobbed occasional balls at the American lines. They never mobilized the sizeable group of Boston Tories or seized Dorchester Heights, which overlooked their anchorage. Washington wanted to put heavy artillery on those heights quickly, because the enlistments of his "Eight-Month Army" would be up by the end of the year, and many of his troops would go home.

British artillery was in place at Fort Ticonderoga, New York, on the southern tip of Lake Champlain. Ethan Allen and his

Green Mountain Boys, along with Benedict Arnold, had captured the fort on May 10, 1775, without firing a shot. Henry Knox volunteered to take a party to bring back the guns. To Knox, there was no "can't be done." Leading a train of 59 iron and bronze cannons of various calibers roped to sledges and dragged by oxen, the bookseller–artilleryman made one of the great winter treks in military history. On March 4, 1776, the guns boomed above Boston for the first time.

As a result, the British garrison and anchorage were indefensible. Patriot gun muzzles thrust through the ports of hand-dug redoubts all along Dorchester Heights. So General Howe gathered his garrison force and many Tory families into transport ships and sailed from Boston for Halifax, Nova Scotia. On March 18, in his first victory, Washington entered the city under a new flag—the Grand Union—made of 13 red and white stripes with a Union Jack in the corner. The colonies—twice victorious—had yet to make the final break.

ARTILLERY FAILURE AT BREED'S HILL

Had the British been able to properly deploy their artillery at Breed's Hill, the outcome might have been different. To bombard the redoubt at the crest, ships' guns were first employed, but the 9–12 pound cannon could not be properly elevated and the target was beyond the 1,200-yard accuracy range of these weapons. Howe's artillery became mired in the marshy ground and then it was discovered the six-pounders had been provided with 12-pound shot. After horrific casualties, grape shot was finally used to carry the American redoubt.

LEFT Two types of cannon balls are shown here. The larger one is solid iron and was used to bowl over soldiers and shatter fortifications. The other is a hollow shot that contained an explosive and fuse; it was usually fired in short-barrel mortars.

DECLARATION OF
INDEPENDENCE—JULY 4, 1776

During the spring of 1776, the words "independence," "separation," and "secession" were spoken in colonial meeting houses and taverns alike. George III had declared the colonies to be in open rebellion. The British garrison in Boston had been forced to decamp to Halifax, and the French were hinting at possible aid against their hereditary enemy. If the will to proceed was wanting, a two-shilling 47-page pamphlet by a recent English immigrant expressed stirring ideas that called for action.

"O ye that love mankind! Ye that dare oppose not only the tyranny but the tyrant, stand forth!"

Thomas Paine's *Common Sense* arrived in Thomas Jefferson's hands that spring as Jefferson prepared to return to Congress at Philadelphia in May. Others were busy rounding up support. John Adams suggested the colonies create independent governments for themselves. North Carolina, Virginia, Georgia, and the New England colonies pressed acceptance of a proposal made on June 7 by Virginia delegate Richard Henry Lee: "That these United Colonies are, and of right ought to be, free and independent states, that they are absolved from all allegiance to the British Crown..." New York abstained; Pennsylvania and South Carolina demurred; while Delaware was split. As the debate continued, Congress created a committee of five to prepare a document declaring independence.

BELOW *Thomas Jefferson wrote the first draft of the Declaration in the rented second floor of this Philadelphia home at Market and 7th Street that belonged to a brick-maker.*

THOMAS PAINE

As a child in England in the 1740s Thomas Paine (1737–1809) failed school, failed apprenticeship at his father's shop, failed in a life at sea, and failed as a tax collector for writing a pamphlet that argued for a pay raise. Fortunately, in 1774 he met Benjamin Franklin who brought him to America. Here, Paine wrote *Common Sense* and *The Crisis*, two works that greatly inspired the founders and the public during the revolution. His most famous work was *The Age of Reason* written in France (1794–96).

This regionally balanced group—John Adams of Massachusetts, Benjamin Franklin of Pennsylvania, Thomas Jefferson of Virginia, Roger Sherman of Connecticut, and the New Yorker Robert R. Livingston—selected Jefferson to draft the declaration.

In a two-storey brick house at Market and 7th Street in Philadelphia, Jefferson's lodgings occupied the entire second floor. There, writing on laid paper on a portable writing desk he had designed, the Virginia planter, scientist, and inventor composed his thoughts to create what he hoped would be "an expression of the American mind."

"We want neither inducement nor power to declare and assert a separation. It is will, alone, which is wanting, and that is growing apace under the fostering hand of our King."

THOMAS JEFFERSON
LETTER TO A BRITISH FRIEND

By June 28, he had a "rough draft," which he shared with Adams and Franklin. After revision, this document was ready for the other committee members. Finally, Jefferson prepared a fresh draft for submission to Congress.

In Pennsylvania's soon-to-be State House, New York's delegates still awaited instructions and Delaware remained split on the resolution for independence. Meanwhile, Caesar Rodney, the third delegate from Delaware, galloped his horse through rain and lightning to cast his vote. Sodden and mud-splashed, he cast it for the resolution. New York eventually voted aye on July 19. Earlier, on July 2, 1776, Congress had approved the resolution for independence. The next day, Jefferson, Adams, Franklin, and other members of the declaration committee presented their document. All that day Congress labored over the declaration's language—deleting its criticism of slavery—and sharpening it. On July 4, President John Hancock and Secretary Charles Thomson signed the draft and it was printed overnight in John Dunlap's print shop. Copies headed out to the other colonies the next morning in the saddlebags of post riders.

On July 8, in front of a crowd in the yard of Pennsylvania's Colony House, John Nixon, a member of the Committee of Safety, read the Declaration of Independence aloud. Reactions were mixed. Amid the cheers and ringing bells, Loyalists and Tories booed and berated. Jefferson's words had captured some of "the American mind," but not all of it, as the next few years would amply demonstrate On the night of July 9, following a reading of the Declaration in New York, Patriots toppled the equestrian statue of George III from its pedestal, broke it up, and sent it on to Connecticut to be melted down and cast into musket balls.

LIBERTY BELL

The Pennsylvania State House needed a bell for its new steeple. The Whitechapel Bell Foundry cast one and, on its first test, it cracked. Philadelphia founders John Pass and John Stow were commissioned to make the bell less brittle and recast it. On their second try, in 1753, it was accepted. The $225 bell weighing 2,044 pounds, and which rings in the key of E flat, is engraved in part "Proclaims Liberty Throughout all the Land..."

DOCUMENT:

2. Thomas Jefferson's first draft of the Declaration of Independence contains scratch-outs, marginal comments by John Adams and Benjamin Franklin and revisions that demonstrate their collaboration of ideas. The concepts are not new, but their combined application added up to treason against the Crown. See envelope, page 19.

BELOW LEFT *This stylized group portrait showing the four committee members handing over the first draft of the Declaration to Congress does not show the exhausted reality of that hot, wet July day.*

BELOW *These ink pots were used at the Continental Congress in Philadelphia to sign and annotate the draft of the Declaration of Independence. Goose quills were the typical writing instrument.*

THE BRITISH SOLDIER

The British army of the eighteenth century was very much conditioned by class. Britain's prisons were also its best recruiting depots and, since a man would rather accept enlistment than face jail, civilians at home dismissed the British "Ranker" as a thug. A private made eight pence a day and, from this, money for clothing, shaving kits, sewing kits, and "health care" was docked. Often the money went into the pockets of the heart of any regiment: the non-commissioned sergeants and corporals, career men who had come up through the ranks and survived. Privates feared their officers and NCOs almost more than the enemy. However, the drill, harsh discipline, cruel punishment, and subordination they meted out also produced the best and most reliable infantry soldier in the European world.

A young boy of 15, hoping to be an officer, began his army career with a commission as ensign, bought for at least £400, although the better the regiment, the higher the cost for commissions. The Footguards charged £900 for an ensign and £3,500 for a captain's commission, compared to £1,500 for a captaincy in an ordinary infantry regiment. If an officer or his family had the means, he could buy his way right up the chain of command. A commission was a lifetime guarantee of employment in the military—unless some gross misconduct forced retirement. For the British, learning by doing from age 15 produced some exceptional commanders.

British soldiers carried 50 pounds of marching order rations, tools, blanket roll, tin or wood canteen and 60 rounds of single ball ammunition on their backs, as well as a .75 caliber Brown Bess musket. Officers carried swords, pistols, and sometimes, long pikes called spontoons or a halberd. Mounted cavalry formed the elite shock troops. Wielding swords, carbine muskets, and dragoon pistols, these dashing horse soldiers were the pride of every army.

Grim-faced British soldiers wheeling into an advancing line with loaded muskets and bayonets made a terrible sight for any opposing army that faced them.

RIGHT *British uniforms were mostly scarlet and white or buff wool cut to fit tight, looking sharp on a parade ground or marching shoulder-to-shoulder towards the enemy.*

BROWN BESS MUSKET

The Short Land Service Musket used by the Regulars of the British infantry during the Revolutionary War had its barrel shortened to 42 inches from the clumsy 46-inch barrel of its predecessor. It weighed about 11 pounds without the 15-inch bayonet. Both muskets were called "Brown Bess," probably from the "browning" of the steel parts to prevent rust and the natural brown stock. The musket could put its smoothbore load into a five-foot diameter circle at 100 yards but it was the weight and density of metal — not well-aimed shots — that cut down the enemy.

THE
CONTINENTAL SOLDIER

Congress authorized the raising of 88 regiments for a Continental Army following pleas from General Washington to not rely on a loose collection of state militias. This Continental Army was to be fashioned on the European model, initially employing British manuals. Not all militias flocked to the colors, some choosing to remain independent. Washington resigned himself to commanding two distinct armies that fought side by side.

A militiaman reported for duty carrying his own smoothbore musket, a shotgun, or occasionally a hunter's long rifle. He needed a cartridge box to hold paper cartridges, or a powder horn and bag to carry balls, and extra flints and tools. He also carried a bladed weapon such as a tomahawk since family muskets could not mount a bayonet for close fighting. A wooden canteen, a haversack for rations, and a blanket completed his equipage. Even drawn up in formation, these "seasonal soldiers" were a motley band.

The Continental soldier generally carried a .69 caliber smoothbore musket about five-feet long that mounted a 15-inch socket bayonet. The arrival of 100,000 1763 French Charleville muskets set the pattern for standard issue. After 1778, training began at Valley Forge, and a manual of arms was established for loading and firing the flintlock musket. This training exercise forced the recruit into the "volley-fire on command" system of stand-up warfare that became streamlined for speed in the field.

1779 · IV · 1783
INFANTRY CONTINENTAL ARMY

LEFT Four uniformed Continental Army "Regulars" in conversation, wearing the common blue coat faced with red, white, or buff, to distinguish State units. The officer (left) carries a "spontoon" spear and wears a short sword.

The Continental Army recruitment quotas were apportioned according to the free population of each state, with regiments varying in size from 700 to as few as 350 men. As Washington took command in Boston, he had no uniforms to distinguish soldier from officer so he designated colored sashes for general officers, colored hat cockades for field officers, and armbands for non-commissioned officers. His own singular sash was pale blue. Even when uniforms became available, the effect was often a hodgepodge. A basic set included a white cotton shirt, waistcoat, regimental coat, and breeches and gaiters or coveralls. White crossbelts carried the bayonet scabbard on one side and the cartridge box on the other. Officers purchased their own uniforms, side arms, and swords.

The American Continental Army and the militias faced the world's greatest army and endured. They were beaten many times, but never defeated.

DOCUMENT:
3. Each Continental Army soldier had to sign an oath of allegiance. The oath bound the soldier to the principles set forth in the Declaration of Independence. This copy was signed and annotated by the army's new commander, General George Washington. See envelope, page 19.

CONTINENTAL UNIFORMS

At the outset, uniforms of the Continental Army were made up of a mix of local militias turned out in civilian knee breeches stockings, buckle shoes, homespun shirts, and wide-brim or tricorn hats of felt, beaver or raccoon. Some states clothed their men in smart unofficial uniforms of various colors. At one point, the French unloaded a mixed lot of blue, brown, and green coat and breeches outfits. By 1779, Washington decreed that blue coats with different color lapel facings would define each unit. However, the frontier sharpshooters kept their buckskins.

THE BRITISH RETURN TO THE COLONIES—1776

When he had occupied Boston on March 18, 1776, General Washington shifted five regiments of New Englanders, Virginia riflemen, Pennsylvanians, and Marylanders along with some artillery to New York. Nathanael Greene had gone ahead to scout Gravesend and the Long Island coast to map possible British landing sites. When the army arrived, they exchanged muskets for shovels and began to dig. They ringed Manhattan and its approaches with redoubts, embrasures, and trenches. Greene, Henry Knox with his big guns, and other commanders created a picture in their minds of what the British would do, and planned accordingly. Washington agreed, and so unwittingly he helped build a trap for his army. Having divided his troops and guns between Long Island and Manhattan, he left Long Island Sound, the Hudson, and East Rivers undefended. This beginner's mistake gave General William Howe, his brother Admiral Sir Richard "Black Dick" Howe, and transports bearing British troops and German mercenaries a pick of landing places.

On June 29, the sun rose on 100 British sail anchored in New York's Lower Bay. Military wisdom dictated that Washington pull his divided and thinly spread army from New York and establish an inland redoubt. But Congress refused to lose face by giving up the city. Washington could have overridden their pleas, but he and his generals decided to stay and fight. American mistakes and British mastery of tactics doomed the defense even as the defenders dug deeper.

While post riders carried the Declaration of Independence throughout the colonies and bells rang and patriots cheered, Congress's army floundered in confusion as it prepared for its first formal battle. Bedeviled by a hundred small details, plagued by the loss of Greene to illness, and struggling with textbook commanders, Washington's unease grew. In trying to defend too much territory with too few assets, a critical breech in the Long Island defenses at Jamaica Plain remained unguarded. Loyalist farmers pointed out the gap to British scouts.

BELOW *Having debarked from transport ships in New York Harbor, British and Hessian troops approach their landing point aboard rowed barges at Gravesend Bay on August 22, 1776.*

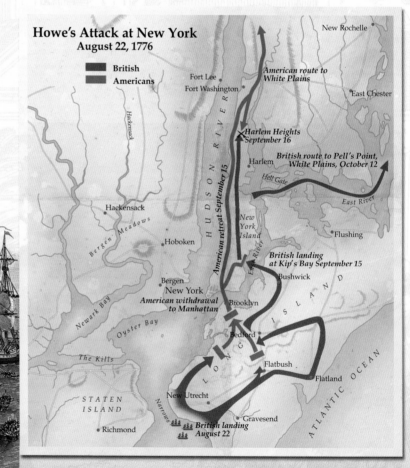

Howe's Attack at New York
August 22, 1776

■ British
■ Americans

New Rochelle

Fort Lee
Fort Washington

American route to White Plains

East Chester

Hackensack

Harlem Heights September 16

Harlem

British route to Pell's Point, White Plains, October 12

Hell Gate

East River

HUDSON RIVER

New York Island

Flushing

Hackensack

Bergen Meadows

American retreat September 15

East River

British landing at Kip's Bay September 15

Bushwick

Hoboken

Bergen
New York

American withdrawal to Manhattan

Brooklyn

LONG ISLAND

Newark Bay

Oyster Bay

Bedford

The Kills

Flatbush

Flatland

ATLANTIC OCEAN

STATEN ISLAND

New Utrecht

Narrows

Gravesend

Richmond

British landing August 22

HOWE BROTHERS

General Sir William Howe (1729–1814) was commander-in-chief of the British army in America from July 1775 to May 1778. His brother, Admiral Sir Richard Howe, older by three years, commanded the British fleet along the American coast. General Howe was opposed to British coercion of North America, and Richard Howe had wanted to lead a peace delegation to the colonies after conversing with Benjamin Franklin. For both, however, duty to the Crown came first.

On August 22, reefed headsails unfurled for steerageway as frigates and bomb ketches, towing 88 barges filled with the first of 15,000 British and German troops, made their way toward Long Island. Martial music from ships' bands and the skirl of bagpipes for the Black Watch troops floated over the scene. On the night of August 26, Generals William Howe, Henry Clinton, and Hessian General Leopold Philipp von Heister marched with 28 pieces of artillery, the 17th Light Dragoons, 71st Highlanders, 33rd West Ridings, the Guards, and 11 other regiments of foot through Jamaica Pass. They proceeded to shoot, carve, and roll up the northern flank of the startled American defenders.

They cut down riflemen—"assassins"—without quarter. Few Americans had bayonets, or knew how to use them. British artillery and sappers blew up the earthworks as the Hessians and Highlanders chopped down surrendering "peasants" and "vile enemies of the King." King George's veteran troops engulfed those patriots who stood up to them. With Knox's heavy guns in the wrong place, the Continental Army and militias were crushed. Only evacuation could save the army, but if the British discovered such a move, surreptitious retreat would turn into rout and slaughter.

Silently, line after line of Continentals disengaged from their positions on the night of August 29. Heroically, John Glover's Marblehead sailors rowed the remaining American army and its supplies from Brooklyn to safety under cover of a rainstorm and fog. The British awoke the next day to find they held a bloody but empty sack.

ABOVE *Once the British occupied New York City a fire of mysterious origins broke out. It was against British interests to burn the city that housed them. Anti-Tory arsonists were suspected.*

LEFT *This map shows the British landing in New York Harbor, their advance across Long Island and their driving of the Americans north, out of the city, towards White Plains, New Jersey.*

BUSHNELL'S TURTLE

On September 7, 1776, David Bushnell slid his peach-shaped submarine seven-feet long and four-feet wide—into New York Harbor to attack British Admiral Howe's flagship, HMS Eagle. The first attack on a warship by a submarine failed. The second attempt to screw the torpedo into the ship's wood hull worked, but the charge failed. Bushnell took his Turtle up to Fort Lee, Washington's headquarters, and tried to sink a frigate. The Turtle was spotted, the torpedo exploded, but it caused no damage.

FROM NEW YORK TO THE JERSEY WOODS—WASHINGTON RETREATS

General Washington and his amateur army had been out-thought, out-fought, and almost crushed into complete surrender. Almost. While he had the bulk of his force ready to continue the retreat toward high ground at Harlem Heights, some 4,000 remained on Manhattan near the battery commanded by Israel Putnam and Henry Knox. Able to sail with impunity, British ships shelled the city and its environs. Barges of light infantry landed alongside the enthusiastic Hessians. Neither Howe, Cornwallis, nor Clinton, who had set up a headquarters in a large house on Murray Hill, thought there was any need to rush. The shabby, untutored Americans were fleeing. Let local commanders have some sport with stragglers and then rest before scooping up the rebel survivors.

Aaron Burr found himself guiding Knox, Putnam, and their commands along a road hidden from British light infantry who were searching for them at the quick march. Screened by dense woods, the uphill trail allowed the wheezing Knox and Putnam to save their troops and avoid capture. As night closed in, the British halted and allowed the Americans to collapse in fatigue atop Harlem Heights.

Surrounded by his exhausted, beaten command, Washington felt he had to hit back if only to raise spirits. Tall, lanky Lieutenant Colonel Thomas Knowlton, who had bloodied the British nose at Breed's Hill, led a picked force of 100 Connecticut Rangers out at dawn in search of the British light infantry. They made immediate contact with 400 troops and let rip a volley. Soon, the Rangers and infantry were exchanging fire, until the honking squeal of bagpipes announced the arrival of the ranks of the Black Watch. Now outnumbered, Knowlton began a fighting retreat. Smelling blood, the light infantry surged forward, followed by the kilted Scots, blowing trumpets as if in a fox hunt and jeering as they ran. Washington ordered 150 Massachusetts men of Nixon's brigade and some rawhide riflemen from the 3rd Virginia to strike the British infantry as it poured into an open field. In line abreast, not from behind walls, the Yankees drew up and blazed away. The light infantry and Black Watch troops stopped short. Now Greene and Putnam struck the fight and soon the British had 5,000 men embroiled. But the Americans stood their ground.

ABOVE *British Officers' metal screw-barrel flintlock pistols. Barrels were threaded to unscrew at the breech to insert the ball and powder. This example was found after the battle of Breed's Hill.*

BELOW *General Charles Lee had been a British officer and expected to command the Continental Army. He ended up third in command and resented the slight. He spread rumors about Washington's lack of ability and was captured by the British in a roadhouse in 1776.*

CHARLES LEE, Esq.
MAJOR GENERAL of the CONTINENTAL ARMY in AMERICA

ABOVE *A period compass set in a protective wood case of a type most officers carried. Since maps were few and good roads fewer still, armies often traveled cross-country or followed rivers. They needed a good compass.*

With British officers and sergeants dropping to rifle shots, and the Yankees' numbers swelling, the redcoats broke and ran. With a "Hurrah!" the mixed lot of Americans pursued them until ordered back when British and Hessian reinforcements arrived. The victorious skirmish had restored a measure of pride to fuel the Continental Army for the long march ahead.

And a long, long march it was, as they were beaten again and again by the British pursuing them up the East River. White Plains, Kyp's Bay, Chatterton's Hill, Pell Point, the loss of Fort Washington and Fort Lee finishing the capture of Manhattan: each engagement added to the litany of despair for those who trudged through the blowing leaves and chill winds of fall.

General Charles Lee, Washington's mocking subordinate, had been taken by the British while dining in a tavern. His army was now far away and without its leader. Desertions whittled away the army as it settled in to winter camp near the west bank of the Delaware River. Howe had called off the chase until spring after establishing outposts in New Jersey to keep an eye on the dwindling American force. As Christmas, 1776 approached, Washington and his officers faced the daunting challenge of feeding, clothing, and sheltering what remained of the patriotic men and boys who had followed them into the snow-covered New Jersey woods.

LEFT *The battle of Long Island showing Maryland and Delaware militias retreating across Gowanus Creek after holding back the British advance. They were outnumbered but kept the retreat as orderly as possible.*

HESSIAN SOLDIERS

"Hessian" soldiers paid by the British as mercenaries during the war were actually recruited from many German principalities. Recruiting officers were active all over Germany. In Hesse-Cassel, the country had been cut up into districts, each of which was to furnish a quota of recruits—as many foreigners as possible in order to spare their own men. Forcible recruiting was forbidden, but spendthrifts, drunkards, and political troublemakers were often forced into the ranks. The colors of the formal uniforms made them easy targets for rebel militia dressed in homespun garb.

FIRST TRENTON—
THEN PRINCETON—1776-1777

RIGHT *This map shows Washington's two-pronged attack on Trenton, which caught the Hessians by surprise. It was backed up by Knox's guns and militia riflemen who covered the escape routes.*

BELOW *In a somewhat fanciful rendering, General Washington crosses the Delaware River with his troops for the dawn attack on Trenton. Hampered by the ice and sleet, the crossing took too long, forcing the daylight battle.*

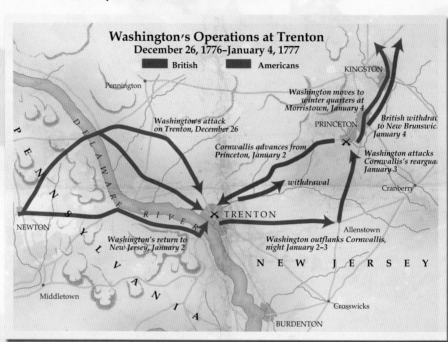

Washington's Operations at Trenton
December 26, 1776–January 4, 1777
■ British   ■ Americans

KINGSTON
Pennington
Washington moves to winter quarters at Morristown, January 4
PRINCETON
British withdraw to New Brunswick, January 4
Washington's attack on Trenton, December 26
Cornwallis advances from Princeton, January 2
Washington attacks Cornwallis's rearguard, January 3
withdrawal
Cranberry
TRENTON
NEWTON
Washington's return to New Jersey, January 2
Washington outflanks Cornwallis, night January 2–3
Allenstown
NEW JERSEY
Middletown
Crosswicks
BURDENTON

The last of the flat-bottomed Durham boats crunched against a creaking pier at McConkey's Ferry on the east bank of the Delaware River. In the early morning darkness of December 26, 1776, General Washington watched the last of his shivering men hustle ashore as John Glover's Marblehead sailor–soldiers exchanged their oars for muskets. Silver cakes of ice flowed past in the black water his army had just crossed. Weeks earlier, he had worked out the plan to strike the Hessian-occupied village of Trenton before dawn and already that plan was falling apart. The river crossing had taken too long. His wretched army, some with rags wrapped around their feet, would face the implacable Hessians in daylight. He mounted up and trotted toward the head of the forming column, speaking to his men as he rode: "For God's sake, keep with your officers."

Washington planned to cross the Delaware at three points to surround the village and block Hessian escape routes. But his generals Cadwalader and Ewing had aborted their crossings due to river ice, leaving Washington's command of 2,400 men unsupported. After traveling five miles into the teeth of a sleet storm, Nathanael Greene and Washington took the ice-slick Pennington Road, while General Sullivan continued to follow the River Road. Four artillery

DRUMS AND MUSIC IN COMBAT

Drums and fifes were not just for morale-stirring entertainment. An officer of the day always had a drummer with him—often as young as 12 years old—to sound the call for alarm, a conference of officers or the "Tattoo." This comes from the Dutch die den tap toe. Taverns must turn off their "taps" so the soldiers would return to camp. During battle, drum calls were used to change marching formations, advance, retreat, or cease-fire.

DOCUMENT:
4. This hand-drawn map of "Prince Town" (Princeton) shows General Washington the layout of buildings and position of British six-pounder cannon batteries. It was prepared by a patriot spy for Washington's attack on Cornwallis's rear guard following the American victory at Trenton. See envelope, page 19.

ABOVE *An artillery crew in action at Trenton. A four-pounder cannon is fired into the Hessians as a ball and powder bag are retrieved from an ammunition box in the foreground. Eighteen cannon crossed the Delaware River with Washington.*

ABOVE *Washington leading his troops in the attack on Princeton made after the victory at Trenton. General Hugh Mercer died as the Americans swept over Cornwallis's rear guard.*

pieces led each column. The sky gradually lightened to a gray, snow-filled overcast as they trudged the last four miles in silence.

The Hessians had been warned of the attack, but doubted the Americans' ability. "If they attack," shrugged General Johann Gottlieb Rall, their commander, "we will give them the bayonet." That morning, while playing cards, he had received a note from a Loyalist and put it in his pocket unopened. So he missed its message: "The rebels have crossed the Delaware to attack Trenton."

At 8 a.m., Greene's men emerged from the woods and faced across a field toward warm houses filled with hot food, blankets, and the hated Hessians. Soaked and freezing, squinting into the cutting sleet, they surged forward in a rushing run called the "long trot."

"Heraus! Heraus!" cried Hessian pickets, as German soldiers piled out of their beds. As the Hessians tried to form up, Henry Knox bellowed "Fire!" and a round of solid shot slammed into their ranks. Hessian band members tried to whistle up a tune, but a barrage of .69 caliber lead greeted them. Sullivan's and Knox's artillery swept the stunned Germans from the main streets, while those who retreated to side streets faced hard-charging Continentals firing as they ran. General Rall tried to rally his men, but fell mortally wounded. Bridges, streets, a near-by apple orchard—all were enfiladed by American fire. Forty-five minutes after the attack began, the Hessians surrendered, leaving 21 dead in the snow, 90 wounded, and 900 as prisoners. No American had been killed in combat, and only four men were wounded.

"The troops behaved like men contending for everything that was dear and valuable," wrote Henry Knox. General Washington granted the men "who crossed the river" a cash equivalent of the spoils seized from the Hessians. Congress, now holed up in Baltimore, was ecstatic. The army savored their victory for only a day and then re-crossed the Delaware.

Shocked into action, Howe sent Cornwallis in pursuit. Again, Washington proved elusive. Decamping at night in front of Cornwallis, the Americans swung around and hit the British rear guard at Princeton. This time, Washington was in the thick of it. Men cheered as he galloped past them, chasing the fleeing British and calling out, "It's a fine fox chase my boys!"

"BUCK AND BALL" FOR CONTINENTAL MUSKETS

In battles between British regulars and Continental troops, the standard weapon was the smoothbore musket. Usually, the hopelessly inaccurate long flintlocks were discharged en masse on command and reloaded as quickly as possible for the next volley. In 1777, however, George Washington authorized the use of one .69 caliber ball and three .31 caliber buckshot in each musket load to increase the power of every American volley. Called "Buck and Ball," the load was never used by the British or French.

WINTER QUARTERS AT MORRISTOWN—1776–1777

As the winter of 1776–77 closed down hostilities, the ragged and exhausted Continental Army shambled into the woods surrounding Morristown, New Jersey, and established their encampment. Except for occasional raids and skirmishes, eighteenth-century warfare generally took a winter time-out. The expense of maintaining an army in the field was prohibitive considering the reduced capabilities of that force due to winter's effect on roads, fields, communications, and morale. Powder became damp in the flintlock's pan, slow matches (cotton wick soaked in lye) failed to stay alight for artillery. Paper-wrapped cartridges became sodden in their boxes. Winter was a time to rest, refit, and take stock.

General Howe retired to New York to pick up his busy social life after the shock of Trenton and Princeton. Word of those sallies failed to rock Parliament in London, which considered the capture of General Charles Lee a great *coup de guerre*, because he was a real commanding officer, not a jumped-up colonel of militia. The American army, it believed, was finished and could be bagged at leisure in the spring.

The land around Morristown had broad fields and plenty of timber to build 14 by 16 foot mud-caulked log huts large enough to house 12 men in each with a fireplace. Other troops were housed in private homes, three or four to a house. With inducements of pay and heartfelt appeals, Washington had persuaded many soldiers whose enlistments were up to remain. He was also determined to maintain discipline and orderly routine in the camp. The construction of a fortification near the town was begun and required considerable labor. It was dubbed "Fort Nonsense" and while it became a supply depot, many considered it a "make-work" project.

Smallpox brought by the soldiers killed a quarter of Morristown's population Sanitation and barnyard notions of cleanliness ensured illness and contagion affected this and future winter encampments.

LEFT *This replica of a soldier's hut built at Morristown, New Jersey, is designed to hold two officers. Each hut had its own entrance and fireplace.*

BELOW LEFT *Interior of a soldier's hut at Morristown, New Jersey, built from original sketches and descriptions. It held 12 men and their belongings. All meals were cooked in the hut as well.*

DISEASE IN WINTER CAMP

The winter camp at Morristown, New Jersey, faced dysentery, rheumatism, and assorted "fevers" associated with bad food, housing, and hygiene, but then smallpox threatened to run rampant through the ranks and the town. A program of inoculation was begun. Washington wrote the Governor of Connecticut, "Inoculation at Philadelphia and in this Neighbourhood has been attended with amazing Success and I have not the least doubt but your Troops will meet the same." Inoculation was also begun at recruiting centers.

LIFE IN WASHINGTON'S MORRISTOWN HQ

The disparity between the crowded huts of the troops in winter camp and the general staff officers' billet at the elegant Ford home in Morristown was necessitated by the administrative needs of the army. Washington's orders had to be hand-copied by a staff of aides. Rooms were needed for conferences and housing for servants. Visiting observers from European countries brought their entourage and needed rooms. And, of course, there had to be room for the Fords and Martha Washington.

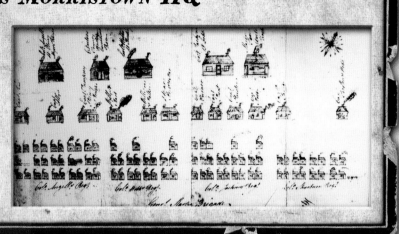

" These are times that try men's souls. The summer soldiers and the sunshine patriot will, in this crisis, shrink from the service of their country; but he that stands it now, deserves the love and thanks of man and woman."

THOMAS PAINE
THE AMERICAN CRISIS, 1776

ABOVE *The imposing Ford mansion, built 1772–74 on a hill in Morristown, was headquarters for General Washington and his staff. The elegant home was needed for visiting dignitaries and their entourage.*

The most common sound heard among the huts and on the parade ground was the hacking cough. Throughout the war more men would die of disease and infection than from fatal combat wounds

At first, food was a problem. Riflemen scoured the countryside for small game, while shotgunners prowled meadows and fallow cornfields. Buoyed by the recent victories, Congress granted Washington the right to commandeer supplies as needed and camp life improved. One day, wagons from the brig *Mercury* arrived, bringing supplies from Nantes, France. They carried bales of clothing, shoes, 364 cases of arms, 11,000 gunflints, and 1,000 barrels of gunpowder from the mills of Lavoisier. Thirty-four more loaded ships were gathering sail from French ports. Diplomatic and commercial discussions with France were paying off.

Washington and his staff quartered in the Arnold Tavern, just off Morristown Green. The constant flow of paperwork required aides-de-camp and secretaries to have a working office space. George was fortunate to have his wife, Martha visit. She radiated a good cheer that was infectious to the men. Later, during the winter of 1779–80, the general's staff moved into the Morristown mansion formerly owned by militia commander Colonel Jacob Ford Jr., who had died campaigning in 1777. The staff lived with the Ford family and was host to a constant visitation by foreign attachés and observers with their retinues.

The winter of 1776–77 proved the Continental Army had a strong, resourceful, and resilient core. Though it still suffered weaknesses of leadership, inexperience with military tactical execution, and a continuing disparity between regular army and militia effectiveness in the field, the army that marched into the spring of 1777 was ready to take the fight to the British once again.

THE FATEFUL DEFEAT OF "GENTLEMAN JOHNNY" BURGOYNE

Philadelphia. Both armies headed toward a confrontation at a picturesque little creek called Brandywine.

Earlier, on May 6, General John Burgoyne had arrived in Quebec to command a force that eventually amounted to 7,213 soldiers and scouts, which was to march south from Canada to join with General Howe, crushing the Americans between them.

The curiosity that had attended General Howe's departure from New York on July 23, 1777, in frigates herding transports packed with thousands of British and Hessians was answered at last. That fleet arrived in Chesapeake Bay on August 22, 1777, only 60-odd miles from Philadelphia.

Meanwhile, the 6,000-strong Continental Army threaded its way through Philadelphia, swinging in step to the tunes of fife and drum toward the invading redcoats amid cheers, and waving hats and kerchiefs. Howe landed his force and stepped off in the direction of

That was the plan as General Burgoyne understood it. His force comprised two columns made up of British and German troops, along with Loyalist scouts, 400 Indian scouts, plus 42 pieces of artillery for each column.

The expedition sailed across Lake Champlain and easily captured Fort Ticonderoga. In high spirits, the clever and confident Burgoyne plunged his troops into the American wilderness of dirt trails, deep ravines, dense woods, and wrecked bridges left by retreating Continentals. These delays allowed even the phlegmatic American General Horatio Gates to gather his forces. Eventually, the British and German columns arrived at the open fields of Freeman's Farm at dawn on September 19.

British skirmishers moved forward toward the south edge of the woods 350 yards distant. They never saw the long Kentucky rifle muzzles poke out from the bushes. They heard instead what sounded like a turkey gobble. The rifles blazed and every officer among the skirmishers fell. The British returned fire at a hopeless range. After a pause, a second rifle volley ripped from the trees. Sergeants dropped and privates collapsed. The hidden riflemen, commanded by General Daniel Morgan, rushed from cover with whoops and yells. The British stood firm and produced a wall of bayonets. The riflemen turned and ran back to the woods. The battle of Freeman's Farm had begun.

Morgan's riflemen picked off cannoneers, sent gunnery officers sprawling, and riddled Burgoyne's coat and hat with holes. With battle-hardened fortitude, the British held their ground, but each day it seemed that more Yankee troops joined the fight on all sides. Up river, along Burgoyne's line of march, General John Stark cut the British river-borne supply line.

GENERAL JOHN BURGOYNE

One of the more flamboyant generals sent to quell the colonies' revolt, John Burgoyne (1722–1792) was outspoken and a non-conformist in his views. His marriage was an elopement, after which he fled to France to avoid debts. "Gentleman Johnny's" military career began with observation of the attack on Breed's Hill and ended with his brilliantly conceived, but poorly executed, attack that ended with surrender at Saratoga. He left the army to write plays and enjoy a literary life.

Out of nowhere, Major General Benedict Arnold arrived and seemed to be everywhere, leading charges and rolling up defenses. For the besieged British and Germans to continue forward was impossible; and then General Stark sealed the road that led back north. After 28 days of bloody combat—the Battle of Saratoga—with his men hungry and being cut to pieces by unrelenting American fire, "Gentleman Johnny" had no choice. On October 17, Burgoyne's army laid down their arms. From his distant headquarters, General Gates arrived at the battlefield to accept the surrender and treated Burgoyne like visiting royalty.

"The fortune of was, General Gates, has made me your prisoner."

GENERAL JOHN BURGOYNE.
SEPT 16, 1777

In the south, General Howe, who never had any intention of joining up with Burgoyne, won a hard-fought battle with Washington's army at Brandywine Creek on 11 September. But the Americans managed to retreat once again with their army intact. Congress fled Philadelphia before Howe moved in for the winter. This time Congress settled in the small town of York. There, the lawmakers continued work on a document called the Articles of Confederation. Most important, however, Burgoyne's defeat led France to shift from logistical support toward a full military and political alliance with this new United States of America.

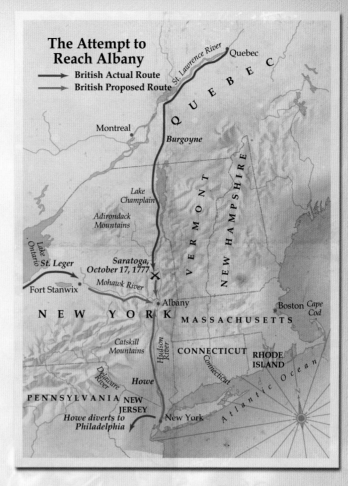

The Attempt to Reach Albany
→ British Actual Route
→ British Proposed Route

ABOVE *General Burgoyne had devised a two-pronged assault, traveling south from Lake Champlain to meet with General Howe coming North. Howe, however, occupied Philadelphia instead and Burgoyne overreached his supply line.*

DOCUMENT:
5. Cobbled together by the Continental Congress—usually on the run during the war—The Articles of Confederation established a weak central government and strong states' rights. The colonies feared a strong central power after so many years under Britain's thumb. See envelope, page 33.

ABOVE *General Burgoyne surrenders to General Horatio Gates, who had little to do with the actual battle. Daniel Morgan and Benedict Arnold were the battlefield commanders.*

GENERAL HORATIO GATES

Brigadier General Horatio Gates (1727–1806) was an excellent administrator, but a luckless commander. He began his career as a British soldier in the French and Indian War and afterwards moved himself and family to Virginia. Washington suggested he join the militia. His ambition was fired by the victory over Burgoyne at Saratoga, but that was followed by a rout of his troops near Camden, South Carolina, in 1780. He later married a rich widow and retired to become a farmer.

INTO VALLEY FORGE
1777–1778

With Congress begging for a winter campaign to oust Howe and his occupying force from Philadelphia, Washington had to consider his army's exhaustion and the meager supplies available to it. He marched into encampment near the village of Valley Forge, Pennsylvania. Though beaten at Brandywine Creek, and forced into yet another retreat before General Howe's troops, morale among the Americans was unusually high.

The army's engineers staked out parallel streets and drill fields and employed soldiers to build 2,000 small huts, each housing 12 men. The sound of axes, hammers, and saws resonated across the rolling hills. The army was short of food, water, and clothing, but not stubborn backbone. Besides their quarters, they managed to build five earthen redoubts and put a sturdy bridge across the nearby Schuylkill River. But for all that, a sentry who greeted Washington one morning had to stand on his hat to keep his bare feet out of the snow.

It was into this frozen outpost that two men came who would leave an indelible mark on the Americans' struggle. Marie Joseph Paul Yves Roch Gilbert du Motier, Marquis de Lafayette, was a wealthy young Frenchman who had left his family and military career to join Washington's army without pay, in hopes of earning a command. His friendship with the general and passion for the Revolution won him respect and a place in the hearts of all American patriots.

BELOW *George Washington passes the colors as the troops are paraded at Valley Forge. Musters on the parade ground, guard duty, and camp routine were kept up despite the cold to keep the army together.*

LEFT *General von Steuben's method of drill taught to the Continental Army was printed in book form for all officers to use. Von Steuben took Prussian rifle and troop movements and simplified them for the colonials.*

VON STEUBEN'S DRILL

Baron Friedrich von Steuben (1730–1794) joined Washington's command at Valley Forge, Pennsylvania, during the winter of 1778 and began training troops. He spoke no English and started small with 100 men. His musket drill broke down the process of loading and firing a musket into 15 precise steps to teach the men discipline that would be applied to his program of troop maneuvers and marching. His manual, Regulations for the Order and Discipline of the Troops of the United States, was published in 1779.

The other man was a former half-pay captain in the Prussian army who had met Benjamin Franklin while the elder statesman was serving as ambassador to France. It is possible that Franklin helped him inflate his dossier to impress Congress and General Washington. So it was that Lieutenant General Baron Friedrich Wilhelm Ludolf Gerhard Augustus von Steuben arrived at Valley Forge to offer his services. He took on the task of teaching the Continental Army to do what it had done since the battle of Breed's and Bunker Hill — how to fight the British. But he taught them to fight as a disciplined army, not as a mob of well-intentioned civilians.

Von Steuben spoke little English, so he started small with a squad of shivering soldiers and had Pierre Duponceau—his French secretary—Colonel John Laurens, or Lieutenant Colonel Alexander Hamilton translate his drills and commands from German into French and then into English. He slowly walked the squad through the commands of loading and firing their flintlocks, taking them through 15 steps from the musket grounded at their side to firing. He taught ranks of soldiers to wheel into line and move as a body,

RIGHT The Marquis de Lafayette came from France and volunteered to fight with Washington. They remained lifelong friends and Lafayette fought significant battles in 1780–81. He became an American hero.

ABOVE *This camp broiler is typical of the mobile kitchenwares carried with the tents and equipment in ox-drawn wagons during troop movements. Made of cast iron, it could serve a squad of soldiers or an officers' mess.*

to master the thrust and parry of the bayonet, and to perform as a military force in the face of Europe's finest army. From squad to platoon to company, the constant drills packed down the snow on the Grand Parade Field. He and Washington, and the young Lafayette watched whole divisions dress ranks, stamp, and half-step to the rattle of drums. Von Steuben's manual of drill became part of every field officer's kit.

As the troops drilled, survived, froze, and some took off for home, the selfless Nathanael Greene accepted Washington's appointment as quartermaster. The same zeal Greene showed in the field, he brought to supplying the thousands of troops. He uncovered long-forgotten stores that been missed by the British during an earlier raid and employed troops to rake and net tons of shad from the Schuylkill River for salting down.

But on May 5, 1778, startling news greeted duty officers that morning. On February 4, France had signed a Treaty of Alliance with the United States of America. They were no longer alone.

VALLEY FORGE CAMP LIFE

Winter camp life at Valley Forge was harsh. The 12-man huts and two-man field officer huts were adequate for shelter, but food rations were slim and winter clothing dependent on private donations, since there was little or no money. Men gathered every morning to hear general orders read, posted guards, and often hunted small game for the pot. Those who could rise from their bunks worked on construction projects. Martha Washington's visits with hot soup were very welcome.

The American alliance with France had an immediate impact. Sir Henry Clinton had just ensconced himself in Philadelphia as Howe's replacement commanding all British forces in North America, when he received orders from London to ship 5,000 of his troops to the West Indies to fight the French. He had to to transport another 3,000 troops to St. Augustine, Florida, to guard against Spain's probably entry into the war. What remained of the Philadelphia occupation force was bound for New York. In the context of British–French global conflict, North America once again became part of a larger whole.

Loyal British Tories had flocked to Philadelphia once the British had taken it. Now the city was to be evacuated and they would be abandoned to the rebels' wrath. Clinton also feared the appearance of French warships, and so decided to send the Loyalists by water routes to British-occupied territory around New York, while he marched his troops overland, crossing the Delaware River into New Jersey on June 18, 1778.

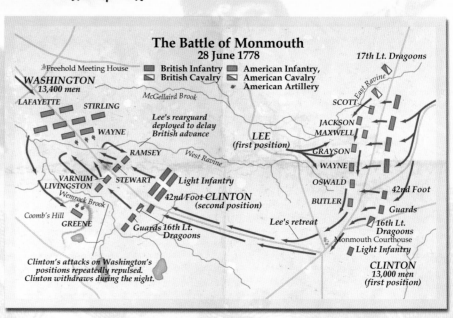

The Battle of Monmouth
28 June 1778

■ British Infantry ■ American Infantry,
◣ British Cavalry ◣ American Cavalry
 ✴ American Artillery

17th Lt. Dragoons

Freehold Meeting House
WASHINGTON
13,400 men
LAFAYETTE   STIRLING
McGellaird Brook
WAYNE
Lee's rearguard deployed to delay British advance
SCOTT
JACKSON
MAXWELL
LEE
(first position)
GRAYSON
RAMSEY   West Ravine   WAYNE
VARNUM
LIVINGSTON   STEWART   Light Infantry
OSWALD   42nd Foot
Wentrock Brook
42nd Foot **CLINTON**
(second position)
BUTLER   Guards
Coomb's Hill
GREENE   Guards 16th Lt. Dragoons   Lee's retreat
16th Lt. Dragoons
Monmouth Courthouse
Light Infantry
CLINTON
13,000 men
(first position)

Clinton's attacks on Washington's positions repeatedly repulsed. Clinton withdraws during the night.

ABOVE *The sea battle between the victorious* Bonhomme Richard, *an old ship given to John Paul Jones by France, and HMS* Serapis *on September 23, 1779, established the Continental navy as more than a handful of privateers.*

By June 1, Clinton's evacuation plan was in Washington's hands. He gave the opportunity to attack Clinton's troops and supply train to General Charles Lee, who immediately turned it down and used every opportunity to slander Washington's leadership and character. Lee was convinced American troops were no match for the British. When the army of 6,000 men was then given to Lafayette and the size of the committed force became known, Lee immediately reconsidered and demanded the command. Obeying protocol, Washington acceded and Lee rode off to seize control.

Though Daniel Morgan shadowed the British, opportunity after opportunity was lost to launch an attack. Lafayette and Anthony Wayne seethed as they listened to British wagons rumble along a road near Monmouth Courthouse. Finally, word reached Washington who ordered Lee to attack immediately. Lee threw up his hands and on June 28 scattered his men all along the British line of march. The result was uncoordinated chaos. Yet the troops trained by von Steuben proved better than their commander. Anthony Wayne's infantry were hotly engaged when elite British cavalry, the Queen's Rangers and 16th Dragoons, thundered forward. Earlier, a cavalry charge had always driven the American rabble to flee. Now, the Continentals wheeled into double lines and delivered crashing volleys that emptied British saddles. "Fix bayonets!" rolled down the line and the Americans advanced, driving the Rangers and Dragoons back upon their own infantry.

At this point, Lee abandoned Wayne, Lafayette, Morgan, and the rest and pounding to the rear called for a full retreat. Lafayette, his sword bloodied, his men fighting toe to toe with the British, looked around to see a solitary figure riding toward him on a white horse. Dusty, streaked with sweat and cantering with his cocked hat held high, George Washington's "presence stopped the retreat," wrote the Marquis. The Americans rallied and held, but could not advance. The magnificently disciplined British had been fighting this kind of battle for 100 years. Aided by darkness, the British wagon train proceeded toward the ships waiting at Sandy Hook.

Washington sent Lee to the rear to await the court martial that would end Lee's career. The Battle of Monmouth ended in a draw, but the Americans had fought on British terms and broken the scarlet line. The main armies would never face each other again bayonet-to-bayonet because the war moved south into other commands. But on the night of June 28, both George Washington and the Marquis de Lafayette fell asleep beneath a gnarled old tree on soil won by the first United States Army.

BELOW *Major John André, a British spy, is captured with the plans to the Hudson River defenses in his boot. His collaboration with American hero General Benedict Arnold rocked the army and General Washington.*

BENEDICT ARNOLD

Benedict Arnold (1741–1801) was an American officer of great personal bravery matched only by his ambition. A man of action and great appetites, he was badly wounded in the leg and blamed Congress for overlooking his claims for advancement. He gave plans of West Point's defense to Loyalist spy John Andreé who was caught and hanged. Arnold fled the United States and led troops against the Americans. He died a pauper in England and was buried in his Continental uniform.

ABOVE *This "Molly Pitcher"—a term used for women who brought troops water—fires a gun during an artillery duel at the Battle of Monmouth. The lower part of her petticoat was probably shot off when a ball went between her legs.*

LEFT *General George Washington confronts General Charles Lee at Monmouth and relieves him of command for retreating. Washington went on to lead the troops back against the British and saved the army once more.*

FIGHT AMERICANS WITH AMERICANS— CAMDEN TO KINGS MOUNTAIN

" From a militia officer waiting to attack: My brave fellows, when you are engaged, you are not to wait for the word of command from me. I will show you but my example how to fight. Fire as quick as you can, and stand your ground as long as you can. "

GENERAL DANIEL MORGAN.
JANUARY 16, 1781

In 1779, the war moved south. General Benjamin Lincoln of Massachusetts, along with a mixed force of militia and Continentals, marched south to support a French attack on a virtually defenseless Savannah, Georgia. The French admiral, Comte d'Estaing, demanded the surrender of the small British garrison in the name of Louis XVI. He then established an elaborate siege of the city, but on October 9 botched the entire attack, incurring 800 casualties. With that dubious accomplishment, and fearing bad weather, d'Estaing packed up his army and sailed away to Martinique, leaving Lincoln to wonder at the value of the French alliance. The American general marched his remaining troops back to Charleston, South Carolina, leaving Savannah in British hands.

Sir Henry Clinton decided an adventure in the south would be good for his army regulars and would allow him to exercise his scheme for using thousands of Tories who, he believed, would flock to the Union Jack. He also gained the assistance of Lieutenant Colonel Banastre Tarleton, the ruthless commander of "Tarleton's Tory Legion," a bloodthirsty

ABOVE *The American frontiersmen—led by elected officers— confront British Major Patrick Ferguson atop Kings Mountain. The major was shot from his horse and the Tories he led finally surrendered.*

DANIEL MORGAN

The "Old Waggoner" was an almost mythical hero of the Revolution. Daniel Morgan (1736–1802) emerged from the wilderness at age 17 and began building a legend that included receiving 500 lashes from the British for striking an officer. Preferring buckskins to a uniform, he and his riflemen achieved fame at Quebec, Freeman's Farm, and his stunning victory at Cowpens. He served a term in Congress, but quit after calling the Jeffersonians, "a bunch of egg-sucking dogs."

RIGHT *This brass and glass pocket-watch was carried though the Revolutionary War by Col. Sylvanus Seeley, Commander of the New Jersey Militia. Good timepieces were needed to co-ordinate troop movements.*

cavalry troop known for scourging rebel civilians as well as enemy troops. Cutting down surrendering soldiers and begging planters alike was dubbed "Tarleton's Quarter."

General Lincoln did not possess Washington's survival skills and bottled up his army in Charleston. Clinton's 10,000 men closed in, while Tarleton hacked shut every escape road. When Lincoln finally surrendered on May 12, 1780, he was treated with complete disdain. Meanwhile, General Horatio Gates brought an army south to attack Cornwallis, who had been building forts in the Carolinas. Gates's poor generalship was consistent with his near-fiasco at Saratoga. On August 16, he blundered into Cornwallis's superior force near Camden, North Carolina. Instead of a prudent withdrawal, Gates attacked. The resulting one-sided slaughter by the Tory Legion left Tarleton's men so exhausted they could hardly lift their swords.

BANASTRE TARLETON

Banastre Tarleton (1754–1833)—whose mother bought his commission in the cavalry for ££800 after he gambled away his fortune—was considered to be the most hated officer in the British Army. Tarleton was an unrepentant man of action who used any means to achieve his goal. In America, he assembled a "British" Legion of Tories; his oppressive tactics offering little or no quarter to his enemies. Lionized back in Britain, he led a long and chaotic life ending in obscurity.

When Gates was eventually located three days after the running battle, his army of almost 3,000 troops had been slashed to a bedraggled band of 700 without food or equipment. American dead amounted to almost 2,000 men, whereas the British had lost only 69 soldiers. Clinton returned to New York, and Cornwallis achieved command in the south. Now he decided to sweep northeast, to quell rebel ardor and build his Tory army. To this end he assigned Major Patrick Ferguson and about 1,000 Tories to secure his left flank.

Uncomfortable at the edge of the Great American Wilderness, Ferguson warned the scattered bands of American trappers, hunters, and "over-the-mountain" men in today's Tennessee that they must join the Crown troops or be invaded. Ferguson sadly miscalculated. Soon, almost 900 hard-living, hard-drinking, sharp-shooting mountain-men were hunting Ferguson's Tory Army. He had gone to ground atop Kings Mountain, a long, narrow plateau-topped ridge.

Cornwallis Retreating!

PHILADELPHIA, April 7, 1781.

Extract of a Letter from Major-General *Greene*, dated CAMP, at *Buffelo Creek, March 23, 1781.*

"ON the 16th Inftant I wrote your Excellency, giving an Account of an Action which happened at Guilford Court-Houfe the Day before. I was then perfuaded that notwithftanding we were obliged to give up the Ground, we had reaped the Advantage of the Action. Circumftances fince confirm me in Opinion that the Enemy were too much gauled to improve their Succefs. We lay at the Iron-Works three Days, preparing ourfelves for another Action, and expecting the Enemy to advance: But of a fudden they took their Departure, leaving behind them evident Marks of Diftrefs. All our wounded at Guilford, which had fallen into their Hands, and 70 of their own, too bad to move, were left at New-Garden. Moft of their Officers fuffered—Lord Cornwallis had his Horfe fhot under him— Col. Steward, of the Guards was killed, General O Hara and Cols. Tarleton and Webfter, wounded. Only three Field-Officers efcaped, if Reports, which feem to be authentic, can be relied on.

Our Army are in good Spirits, notwithftanding our Sufferings, and are advancing towards the Enemy; they are retreating to Crofs-Creek.

In South-Carolina, Generals Sumpter and Marian have gained feveral little Advantages. In one the Enemy loft 60 Men, who had under their Care a large Quantity of Stores, which were taken, but by an unfortunate Miftake were afterwards re taken.

**Publifhed by Order,
CHARLES THOMSON, Secretary.**

$§§ Printed at N. Willis's Office.

ABOVE *A propaganda broadside printed as Cornwallis moved his troops south overland after Monmouth and Kings Mountain. American Generals Greene and Lafayette harassed the column as it moved.*

Ferguson's Tories had been taught to fight like British regulars with Brown Bess muskets and bayonets. The mountain-men under Colonels Isaac Shelby and "Nolichucky Jack" Sevier were long-range riflemen who used knives and tomahawks for close work. Indian war whoops began the battle—on October 7, 1780—and the buckskin-clad warriors stormed the plateau from all sides. Firing as they climbed, the long-riflemen aimed low and sheared away line after line of Tories, while musket volleys hissed high above the mountain-men's heads. Tory bayonet charges met killing fire. Soon the riflemen gained the top of Kings Mountain and the Tories began surrendering. Unable to accept surrender "to such banditti," Ferguson wheeled his horse and charged with sword raised. He and the men who followed him were shot to pieces by 50 rifles. The British concept of "fighting Americans with Americans" had failed miserably here.

DOCUMENT:

6. The Treaty of Alliance brought France into the Revolution on the United States' side. The French could now openly back the colonies with troops, ships, and weapons, where before they had been forced to aid the United States covertly. Burgoyne's defeat sealed the deal. See envelope, page 33.

COWPENS
1780

LEFT *Colonel Tarleton's Dragoons are surprised by American cavalry commanded by Colonel William Washington. The British cavalry were sweeping down on retreating militia when Washington successfully counter-attacked.*

GENERAL CHARLES CORNWALLIS

General Cornwallis (1738–1805) came from a classic upper-class background, becoming an ensign in the 1st Grenadier Guards before his 18th birthday. He opposed the Parliamentary measures that caused the Revolution, but once sent to the Colonies as a major general, he did his duty as an excellent and insightful commander. Following his defeat at Yorktown, he pursued a diplomatic career, ending his days in India as governor-general. He died there at Ghazipur on Oct. 5, 1805.

In December 2, 1780, Major General Nathanael Greene inherited a wretched command from the unfortunate Horatio Gates. Its paper strength was 2,500, but only 1,500 showed up for duty, and only 800 of those were equipped for the field. Greene moved the mob into a "camp of repose" 60 miles southeast of Charlotte, North Carolina. There, he and some very able officers began to whip them back into shape. Among these officers were Colonel John Eager Howard, Polish engineer Thadeusz Kosciuszko, the able cavalry commander William Washington and—drawn from his 1779 retirement—the "Old Waggoner" Daniel Morgan. Crippled by arthritis and sciatica, he accepted the rank of brigadier general and reported for duty.

Greene divided his already small force into three commands. Each unit could strike at Cornwallis's communications outposts, ambush his supply lines, or harass his flanks. Whichever unit Cornwallis moved against, Greene could strike elsewhere. Puzzled by this information from Tory scouts on the divided command, Cornwallis picked up the challenge and divided his own command, attacking each of Greene's three groups. He chose Banastre Tarleton with his British Legion, dragoons, Highlanders, infantry, light artillery, and a group of Tories totaling 1,100 men to dispose of Morgan's "nuisance."

The towering, burly Morgan, clad in buckskins, chose his fighting ground with care; a sprawling cow pasture, known locally as "cowpens," with no trees to inhibit movement of troops or cavalry, but with hills and depressions perfect for concealment. On January 16, as Tarleton's exhausted troops bedded down a short distance away after a killing march, Morgan visited every camp-fire to explain his plan and cheer his men.

Tarleton began his advance at 3:00 a.m., stripped of baggage and ready for battle. Tory scouts brought back news that militia had been sighted and that Morgan's main body was nearby. Tarleton was elated and spurred ahead with 50 dragoons. They spotted the usual ragged mob of militia, swung into line and trotted forward. Gunfire sheeted across the tall grass from Morgan's picked marksmen. Fifteen saddles emptied and Tarleton halted. He waved forward his infantry who came at the double. The militia waited, and then a second volley shattered the sound of running boots and jingling equipment. A dozen British officers and NCOs dropped. The militia ran to the rear through a second line of riflemen. Encouraged, Tarleton urged his dressed ranks forward. The second line fired at 50 paces. British soldiers toppled and recoiled. The first line had reloaded and added a volley that further bloodied the ground. Then all the militia ran, splitting left and right around a rising hill. With a collective roar, the enraged British infantry broke ranks and charged up the rise. Tarleton and his cavalry swept forward.

British troops surged over the crest and into the grim-faced ranks of Marylander and Delaware Continentals arrayed in parade ground lines. Howard's first volley decimated the regulars. Tarleton's Legion galloped in to be hit on their flank by Colonel William Washington's dragoons and Lieutenant Colonel James McCall's sword-wielding cavalry. Virginia riflemen raked the other flank. Howard's final volley at point-blank range, followed by a bayonet charge into the bloody mass, finished it.

Abandoned by his Legion, Tarleton escaped, but he was broken that day. Cornwallis pursued Greene's army, but lost a race to the Dan River across which Greene escaped, ready to inflict further destruction on Cornwallis's line of communications. The two generals dueled across the south until Clinton ordered Cornwallis to send troops to New York to frustrate any French attack. Cornwallis did so, and found himself holing up in a Virginia coastal village on the James River called Yorktown.

THE FRIEND OF WASHINGTON

LIEUTENANT COLONEL PATRICK FERGUSON

A distinguished leader of Tory troops and of his own "Sharp Shooters," who used his patented rifle. Ferguson (1744–1780) tells of confronting two Continental officers on September 7, 1777. One was very tall and distinguished on a bay horse, wearing a cocked hat. Ferguson's men could have cut them down, but he ordered their surrender. The tall officer wheeled his horse and galloped away. Ferguson could not shoot him in the back. Later, he learned the officer was probably George Washington.

LEFT *Tadeusz Andrzej Bonawentura Kosciuszko, a Polish engineer, used his skills and the rebels' proven ability to dig and throw up formidable earthworks to defeat Barry St. Leger's support of Burgoyne's army and deny British troops the Hudson River's west bank.*

Lieutenant Colonel Francis Marion entertains a captured British officer at an American camp. Marion's guerilla tactics and raids, using the swamps for cover and rivers as highways, harassed the British.

YORKTOWN 1781

By 1781, the American army was, as Washington wrote, "at the end of our tether." Washington was convinced he could not defeat the British unless by some bold stroke of luck. Curiously, the British were coming to that same conclusion regarding their own chances of victory. The simple thrashing of some ranting rabble had turned into seven years of bloody campaigning and still the American army stood undefeated. It had been beaten and beaten, chased and beaten again, but refused to capitulate. Instead, the provincials had chastened several of Britain's finest general officers and had routed some of the finest regiments of foot and horse. And now the opportunistic French had come in with their equally opportunistic allies, the Dutch and Spanish, sniffing for plunder at Britain's expense. With the fleet stretched thin and British admirals seeing French sail stalking every possession and port in the empire, prolonging the North American adventure seemed to be a bad investment.

And yet Lieutenant General Lord Cornwallis saw a glimmer of hope, and in late 1780 he drove his army into Virginia, the heart of the Americans' economy and supply lines, and a center of radical resistance. Greene's army was still licking its wounds from their last confrontations. Only the Marquis de Lafayette and Anthony Wayne had small forces in the field, and Cornwallis kept these at bay using the services of infamous Lieutenant Colonel Banastre Tarleton's dragoons and through superior numbers of infantry and guns.

Over in New York, Lieutenant General Sir Henry Clinton fumed. He disputed Cornwallis's method of taking the war to the Americans. Resolving to keep him under control through communication by sea, Clinton ordered Cornwallis to select a headquarters on the Virginia coast. Cornwallis chose Yorktown, Virginia, which was set on a short spur of land flanked by the James and York rivers, with its back to Chesapeake Bay and the Atlantic Ocean beyond. There, he felt safe. After all, Britannia ruled the waves. He had little to fear from a direct attack over land by the Americans. Some redoubts and trench work to the south seemed adequate defense.

What Cornwallis did not know was that the French general, Comte de Rochambeau had marched his French troops from Rhode Island to link up with Washington's command. Nor did Cornwallis know French Admiral Comte de Grasse and a fleet of 28 sail were heading for Chesapeake Bay. When 3,000 French troops were landed on August 30 to swell Lafayette's command, and both Washington and Rochambeau arrived with their combined force, Cornwallis found his army of 7,800 facing 16,000 troops, artillery, and engineers,

BATTLE OF THE VIRGINIA CAPES

The sea battle off the Virginia Capes on September 5, 1781, between French Admiral François Comte de Grasse and British Admiral Sir Thomas Graves decided the fate of Yorktown. Graves's command was outnumbered by the disorganized French and his ships had the wind advantage. Unfortunately the British commanders failed to exploit this, allowing the French to regroup. Subsequent ship action battered the British. His fleet low in morale and in physical disarray, Graves allowed the French to return to the siege of Yorktown.

LEFT *Colonel Alexander Hamilton led the American troops in the capture of British Redoubt #10. They carried the position, making the British defenses impossible to maintain.*

SURRENDER OF CORNWALLIS,
AT YORK-TOWN V? OCT. 1781.

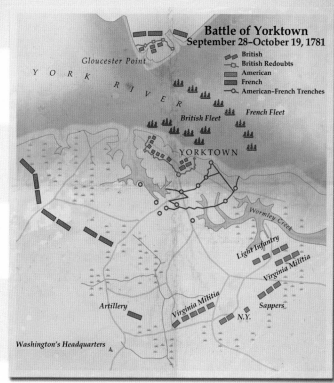

Battle of Yorktown
September 28–October 19, 1781

British
British Redoubts
American
French
American–French Trenches

Gloucester Point

Y O R K — R I V E R

British Fleet   French Fleet

YORKTOWN

Wormley Creek

Light Infantry

Virginia Militia

Artillery   Virginia Militia   N.Y.   Sappers

Washington's Headquarters

ABOVE *British General O'Hara surrendered to General Lincoln as Washington and Rochambeau watched. Cornwallis was not present and all the officers were mounted.*

RIGHT *A map showing the French fleet blockading the bay at the York River, keeping supplies and reinforcements from reaching Cornwallis's army. The Americans and French had encircled Yorktown with gun batteries.*

who were already busy snaking trenches through the sandy soil toward his redoubts. He must have looked longingly out to sea as the first artillery barrage fell on Yorktown.

French guns and the heavy guns of myopic, overweight Henry Knox hammered the British trench works and the town. Other faces were part of the encircling army who had stayed with the cause since Breed's and Bunker Hill in '75. In a bold sally, Captain Alexander Hamilton led his command in a rush that captured a key British redoubt. The sound of shovels filled the night as the allied trenches and guns moved closer. General Howe would have remembered: "Never give the rebels time to dig."

On September 5, Admiral de Grasse sortied out from Chesapeake Bay and turned away an inferior force led by British Admiral Graves. With Clinton holed up in New York and every escape route closed, Cornwallis asked for a truce on October 17. Two days later, his army marched into captivity between silent ranks of American and French soldiers. Standing with the American officers, Lafayette remarked: "Sir, the play is over."

DOCUMENTS:

7. British General Cornwallis penned this letter to General George Washington on October 17, 1781, asking for a truce. Cornwallis had sent another letter to British General Clinton in New York, stating the impossible position of the Yorktown fortifications.

8. The Treaty of Paris, signed in 1783, ended all conflict between Great Britain and the United States, and introduced the former British colonies to the world as a free and independent country. See envelope, page 33.

ARTILLERY SIEGE

During the siege of Yorktown, Virginia in September–October 1781, French and American troops used howitzers and mortars to lob heated shot and explosive shells into the town and the British redoubts. Starting at 1,000 yards, Allied gunners used trenches to move the guns forward. The British 44-gun frigate *Charon* and several buildings were set afire. By October 17, a Hessian soldier wrote: "...There was nothing to see but bombs and cannon balls raining down on our lines."

CREATING A COUNTRY FROM SCRATCH

ABOVE *Alexander Hamilton, together with James Madison, favored a strong central government. He was a financial genius of his time, had a mercurial temper. Hamilton and Madison wrote what came to be* The Federalist Papers *to explain their position.*

The United States of America began as a huge experiment. The European world took a long look at the motley collection of states, each scrambling for itself in a confederation held together by a set of articles so limited in its power structure that each state virtually became a nation unto itself. The Comte de Vergennes, France's foreign minister, and the United States' champion at Louis XVI's court, surveyed the tragic tangle that was America's post-war government and commented: "the American Confederation has a great tendency toward dissolution."

Each state legislature began testing the waters and either followed the passionate lead of those such as New York's Alexander Hamilton who preached for strong central government, or held states' individual rights to be sacred and sought to minimize the central grip on power. Using Thomas Paine's *Common Sense* and Jefferson's Declaration of Independence as models wherein troubles flowed from a tyrannical monarch and a corrupt central government, the Articles of Confederation stripped away most executive and central authority. Great Britain was convinced that the United States was impotent and falling apart. It sent no minister to New York where the Congress met, and John Adams, minister to Great Britain, received a cool, almost dismissive reception. Foreign ministers were required to present their portfolios to the governors of all 13 states. Trade tariffs between states hampered interstate commerce. Talking to the states about raising funds to pay debts and fix roads or ports was, Robert Morris said, "like preaching to the dead." During a financial depression in Massachusetts, a taxpayers' revolt was suppressed by the state militia.

ABOVE LEFT *Benjamin Franklin is greeted in Philadelphia on September 14, 1785, by his daughter Sarah Bache, her family, and friends on his return from France after a stay of more than eight years.*

With virtually all the Founding Fathers out of the country, or back in their home states, only one veteran legislator and diplomat, John Jay, argued for abandoning sectional self-interest for a strong central government. James Madison seized on a Virginia convention organized to regulate commerce with Maryland to suggest a more encompassing purpose involving all 13 states. Ultimately, with the blessing of Congress, 55 representatives from 12 states—Rhode Island boycotted—made their way to Philadelphia. On May 25, 1787, the Convention was gaveled to order, and after four months of debate and compromise, the delegates decided to replace the

Articles of Confederation with a more centralized United States Constitution. On September 17, they adjourned and headed for the City Tavern. Selling it to the folks back home would be an even harder job.

One by one, in sessions filled with passion, oratory, slander, invective, the states finally ratified the document. When the deed was done, friends of the Constitution organized celebrations in major towns and state capitals. Following the jubilation in Philadelphia, patriot physician Benjamin Rush wrote John Adams that, at last, the Constitution "…made us a nation."

In September 1789, at the first meeting of the new Congress, James Madison presented 10 amendments called The Bill of Rights (passed on September 25, 1789), which chiefly guaranteed individual rights, as well as freedom of speech and religion. Of the three branches of government—legislative, judicial, and executive—the executive had been the object of the most suspicion. However, an august presence had been among them throughout the process. Now, all heads turned toward the man who had kept the army together and hope alive during the Revolution. Following a popular election, George Washington was unanimously elected by the Electoral College as the first president of the United States. He arrived in New York for his inauguration on April 30, 1789. With John Adams as Vice President and a congress made up of some of the most brilliant minds of the era, the American government became as much explorers as those pioneers who were crossing the Appalachian Mountains to see what was on the other side.

BELOW LEFT *By 1783, the United States Army was disbanding, as armies in the field turned in their muskets, drums, and accoutrements. Units paraded for the last time, said their farewells and headed home. Congress had no money and farms needed planting.*

JAMES MADISON

James Madison (1751–1836) was a well-read lawyer and leader of the Virginia Assembly. He was key to the debate on a strong central government versus a loose confederation of states. Madison, along with Alexander Hamilton and John Jay, anonymously published The Federalist Papers, which moved many states' representatives to agree to the adoption of a strong United States Constitution. Madison became the fourth president in 1809.

DOCUMENTS:

9. After living for 10 years with the ineffectual Articles of Confederation, a new constitution was created and debated in 1787. Supporters of states' rights fought Federalists over the powers of a central government. The Constitution of the United States was the outcome.

10. The Bill of Rights was penned by the "Father of the Constitution," James Madison. It represented the first 10 amendments to the main document. They outline the freedoms and responsibilities of individuals legally protected by the government.

11. In 1789, George Washington was unanimously elected President by the representatives of the 13 colonies. He took the oath of office in New York City, then the nation's capital. He wrote an inaugural address because he was expected to say something after the ceremony. For all, see envelope, page 43.

WASHINGTON THE HOMEBODY

Although he had no children of his own, George Washington was a devoted husband and father to his stepchildren. Before marrying Martha Custis, George had enlarged Mount Vernon into a two-and-a-half story home. She and her two children, Jacky and Patsy, arrived in April 1759. Patsy died there in 1773 and the Washingtons raised two of their grandchildren, Eleanor and George, at Mount Vernon. After his presidency, George and Martha lived in the homestead from 1797 until his death in 1799.

LEFT *George Washington's gold-headed walking cane. He carried this stick through his civilian life and presidency. Tall, elegant, and serene, he was an ideal choice as President of the Constitutional Convention.*

AMERICA LOOKS WEST FOR ELBOW ROOM

BELOW *Bridal Veil Falls, tumbling 620 feet down the canyon walls of what became Yosemite National Park in the Sierra Nevada mountains, was one of the wonders westward travelers discovered as they followed the footsteps of Lewis and Clark.*

During the tumultuous times the United States experienced under the government of the Articles of Confederation, Spain was the largest landholder in North America. The King of Spain owned Florida, coastal land in Alabama, Mississippi, and the banks of the Mississippi River from Natchez to the Gulf of Mexico, everything south of Canada and west of that river. Spain wanted to control the Mississippi River and its port on the Gulf of Mexico as a barrier against any expansionist ideas their new ally, the United States, might entertain. East of the river, many of the states planned to turn the waterway—open or closed to navigation—to their financial gain.

But by the time the Americans had created their Constitution and the new Congress and President George Washington were taking office, the French were wresting their government away from King Louis XVI in the Revolution of 1789. Also at this time, a certain young French officer of Corsican birth told his fellow officers that: "Revolutions are ideal times for soldiers with a bit of wit and the courage to act."

Soon, the new French Republic had declared war on Britain and Spain. This war split American sympathies, but being non-combatants, their primary interest was how to avoid damage and somehow come out ahead. This the United States managed with the Treaty of San Lorenzo, signed on October 27, 1795. The border with Spanish Florida was fixed at the 31st parallel and the Mississippi River was opened for American trade to the Gulf of Mexico and beyond. However, by the turn of the century, the French had negotiated Louisiana from Spain and that Corsican officer—Napoleon Bonaparte—needed cash. President Thomas Jefferson, former minister to France James Monroe, and the current resident French minister Robert R. Livingston, offered to accommodate Napoleon.

On July 14, 1803, a courier handed President Jefferson an envelope containing the Louisiana Purchase, which had been signed on April 30, together with Livingston's and Monroe's cover letter. The letter noted, apologetically that they had managed:

MERIWETHER LEWIS

Virginian Meriwether Lewis (1774–1809), the son of a wealthy father, had an adventurous disposition. In 1794, he volunteered with the troops who put down the Whiskey Rebellion in western Pennsylvania. His natural curiosity led him west where he learned Indian languages and woodcraft. A neighbor of Thomas Jefferson, he became the president's personal secretary and was invited to explore the territory of the Louisiana Purchase. Following that triumph, he became moody and withdrawn, dying from a self-inflicted pistol shot in a tavern near Nashville, Tennessee.

PRESIDENT THOMAS JEFFERSON

When Thomas Jefferson (1743–1826) became the United States' third President in 1801, the formality of the office, if not its importance, took a decided turn. A quiet and scholarly man, his interests included agriculture, horticulture, archeology, philosophy, architecture, and invention. The presidential residence lost its armed guard at the front entrance and the president himself often answered the door, sometimes in a robe and slippers.

DOCUMENT:

12. President Thomas Jefferson wrote this letter to his then secretary, Meriwether Lewis, requesting that Lewis take charge of creating the "Corps of Discovery" and lead a party of explorers west to follow the Missouri River to—if possible—the Pacific Ocean. See envelope, page 43.

BELOW LEFT *Standing on the back of his pony, a war chief in full headdress warns the scout for a distant wagon train that entry into the tribe's land will require some negotiation—usually the transfer of a few horses or muskets.*

BELOW RIGHT *The romantic image of the trailblazing adventurer of the early nineteenth century was only partly true. Life was hard on the prairie or in the mountains and the basic tools of defense, medicine, and nutrition left a lot to be desired.*

"An acquisition of so great an extent [that] was, we well know, not contemplated by our appointment." For $15 million that "acquisition" amounted to over 529 million acres—at three cents an acre—of western land. Curiously, Napoleon sold what he did not yet own. A month after the purchase was signed, Spain formally ceded the land to France.

The American odyssey was turning west and this purchase threw open the gates. On January 18, 1803, three months before the purchase was signed, President Jefferson sent a secret letter to Congress asking for $2,500 to fund an expedition that would cross the Mississippi River, head west and keep going. "The interests of commerce," he wrote, "place the principal object within the constitutional powers and care of Congress. That it should incidentally advance the geographic knowledge of our own continent," he added, "can not but be an additional gratification."

Lieutenant Meriwether Lewis, naturalist, Indian fighter with a knowledge of their languages and, in 1801 Jefferson's private secretary, had begun extensive preparation with known travelers' accounts and maps of Louisiana.

RIGHT *Elbow room meant braving contact with the Indians, who were still touchy about their treatment by both the Americans and the British before and after the war. Warnings, like this booklet, were widely circulated.*

Meticulously, Lewis planned a two-year journey into the uncharted west. He called upon an Army friend, William Clark, to accompany him and the "Corps of Discovery." Clark was a brilliant choice. An engineer with knowledge of topography and surveying, he also knew and respected many of the Indian tribes they would encounter. As Lewis and Clark prepared to move out, other Americans loaded wagons, hitched up their oxen, and added their number to the great westward migration.

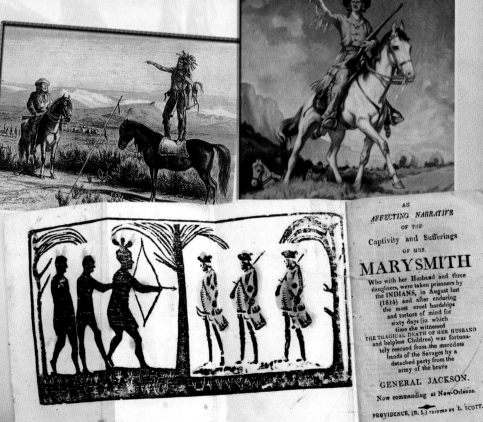

AN AFFECTING NARRATIVE OF THE Captivity and Sufferings OF MRS. MARY SMITH Who with her Husband and three daughters, were taken prisoners by the INDIANS, in August last (1814) and after enduring the most cruel hardships and torture of mind for sixty days (in which time she witnessed THE TRAGICAL DEATH OF HER HUSBAND and helpless Children) was fortunately rescued from the merciless hands of the Savages by a detached party from the army of the brave GENERAL JACKSON. Now commanding at New-Orleans. PROVIDENCE, (R. I.) PRINTED BY L. SCOTT.

THE UNITED STATES ASSERTS ITSELF—THE TRIPOLITAN WAR

STEPHEN DECATUR

One of the most important naval commanders in United States history, Stephen Decatur (1779–1820) became master of the frigate United States after serving on her as an ensign. He captained the ship to victory over the British frigate Macedonian in the War of 1812. Later, he was victorious over the Barbary pirates in the Mediterranean and made his famous, hubris-laden toast: "Our country! In her intercourse with foreign nations may she always be right; but our country, right or wrong!"

Many things were on Thomas Jefferson's mind as he walked the two blocks from his boarding house to the Capitol building on March 4, 1801. First off, his legs itched. He was the first president to be sworn in wearing long pants, instead of knee britches. Next, he wanted to heal the wounds of the election, the personal attacks, and harsh invective. And finally, there were the Barbary pirates.

Since the end of the revolution in 1783, American shipping in the Mediterranean had been victimized by pirates. Using long galleys powered by oars and lateen sails, the corsairs staged their raids from bays and coves along the shores of Morocco, Algeria, Tunisia, and Tripolitania. Armed with swivel guns mounted fore and aft, they cowed unarmed merchant vessels and steered sailors and cargo into captivity to be sold as slaves or ransomed. To avoid these attacks, countries that were already involved in conflicts elsewhere found it easier to pay tribute to the Mediterranean pashas who controlled the pirates and to concentrate on one war at a time.

By 1803, the United States Navy had a squadron of six heavy frigates. The idea of paying tribute to the Bashaw Yusuf Karamanli of Tripolitania raised the hackles of President Jefferson, Secretary of State James Madison, and Secretary of War Henry Dearborn. By the time Jefferson was sworn in, the United States had paid over $2 million to the pirates' masters.

Whenever the Bashaw deemed payments were too small or late, he would send an overwhelming platoon to the American Consul and chop down the flagpole. The insult to American colors was interpreted in the United States as an act of war.

Commodore Richard Dale, with a small fleet of frigates, suggested convoying American merchant ships from port to port. Meanwhile, the sloop *Enterprise* was returning from Malta when a Barbary corsair, the *Tripoli*, appeared hull up on the horizon. Flying a British ensign to draw the pirate closer, Lieutenant Andrew Sterrett waited until the captain of the corsair, Admiral Rais Mahomet Rous, called across that he was hunting Americans. Sterrett ran up the Stars and Stripes and opened fire. American gunnery tore into the 14-gun warship. When Rais tried to grapple, US Marines swept the deck with musket fire. Rais lowered his colors in surrender, but when Sterrett moved in to accept, the admiral raised them again and fired. Sterrett pounded the pirate into a sinking wreck, killed most of the crew, and left Rais bobbing in the sea beneath a jury-rigged mast.

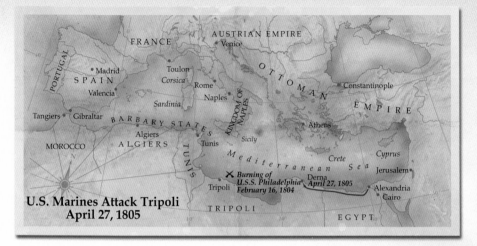

**U.S. Marines Attack Tripoli
April 27, 1805**

When the defeated admiral arrived in front of the Bashaw, the humiliated monarch sent the wretched Rais through the streets of Tripoli riding backwards on a jackass with sheep entrails wrapped around his neck, and later awarded him 500 lashes on the soles of his feet.

With diplomacy exhausted, Commodore Edward Preble appeared off Tripoli with a squadron of American warships. During the maneuvering, the frigate *Philadelphia* ran aground. It was towed away by the Bashaw's sailors and its crew imprisoned for a $200,000 ransom. The answer was a daring raid by Lieutenant Stephen Decatur on the night of February 16, 1804, during which the captured frigate was burnt to the waterline. Preble's squadron then began a crashing bombardment of Tripoli.

As the guns continued to roar, the United States launched land and sea attacks, including an assault by United States Marines leading a polyglot force of mercenaries, who seized the harbor fortress of Derna on April 25, 1805. With the US navy kicking at his front door and Marines swarming from the desert at his back, the Bashaw reached for his pen. On June 4, 1805, he signed a treaty in the main cabin of the frigate *Constitution* giving American shipping unmolested use of the North African ports.

ABOVE *William Bainbridge, captain of the frigate* George Washington, *and later the* Philadelphia, *delivers tribute money from the United States to the Dey of Algiers in 1800. He was later imprisoned with his crew.*

PIRATE GALLEY

The pirates of the Barbary Coast employed slender oar-powered galleys rowed by slaves, which easily closed on merchant ships that relied on the soft breezes crossing the Mediterranean Sea. Armament consisted of swivel guns mounted along the sides and one or two big guns in the bows. But their chief weapon was the crew, often numbering 100 or more, armed with curved swords, pistols, and muskets, who swarmed aboard their victims' ships.

A SENSELESS DUEL & THE CORPS OF DISCOVERY

The nineteenth century was still young when two men faced each other bound by old-world ritual and two others stepped off into a new world of discovery.

On July 11, 1804, Alexander Hamilton faced Aaron Burr at an early morning duel in a field in Weehawken, New Jersey. Hamilton had fought with distinction in the Revolution as a captain of artillery. The intellect of the brilliant former Secretary of the Treasury was vast, and determined when challenged. Aaron Burr served four years in the Revolution, developed into a canny politician, and became Thomas Jefferson's vice president in 1800. Also brilliant and ambitious, he was considered by Hamilton and many of his contemporaries to be a political schemer.

Hamilton's and Burr's personal antagonism erupted in an exchange of letters so insulting that only a duel could save each man's "honor." They faced each other from 10 paces that summer morning, and in an exchange of shots two promising careers were shattered. Hamilton fell with a bullet lodged against his spine, to die next day in excruciating pain. Burr was indicted for murder and fled. His reputation shattered, he became involved in a scheme to set himself up as Aaron I, emperor of the West. After numerous failed European ventures, he returned to the US, often using the name Aaron Edwards, and lived in obscurity until his death in 1836.

On May 30, 1804, Captain Meriwether Lewis, Captain William Clark, and a collection of rugged adventurers calling themselves the Corps of Discovery began the exploration of the territories of the new Louisiana Purchase. This acquisition of this tract of land had virtually doubled the size of the United States. During two years of planning, Lewis, with meticulous attention to detail, attempted to account for every contingency. Gunpowder for the expedition's rifles was stored in cans made of lead.

SACAGAWEA
INDIAN INTERPRETER

On Lewis and Clark's exploration of the Louisiana Purchase, Sacagawea's husband, Toussaint Charbonneau, was hired as an interpreter. Sacagawea came along as an unofficial member because Lewis and Clark thought she could help speak to some of the Indian tribes and also assist with trading horses from her native Shoshone tribe. Sacagawea (1787–1812) had been stolen by the Hidatsa from her native Shoshone tribe. In Hidatsa her name was Tsi-ki-ka-wi-as, "Bird Woman" In Shoshone, her name means "Boat Pusher."

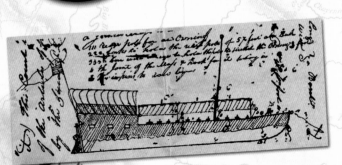

ABOVE *Lewis had a large keelboat constructed to carry the expedition's considerable supplies down the Missouri River. Powered by oars as it headed upstream, the boat had a shallow draft. William Clark drew this sketch.*

LEFT *Meriwether Lewis and William Clark lead their "Corps of Discovery" on the Lower Columbia River. Sacagawea helped communicate and the Black crew member, York, fascinated the Indians.*

Millions of American bison—called buffalo—roamed the western plains. They were used by the Indian tribes for food and clothing. Early settlers depended on their meat, their hides and their dried dung—buffalo chips—to build fires. The animals were hunted almost to extinction.

Once opened, the powder was shared out and the can melted down to make bullets. To conserve powder, an air rifle was included in their arsenal, as well as a small cannon to assert their authority. Twenty-one barrels of flour and 193 pounds of "portable soup" were stowed in sealed cans. The most important camp tool was the tomahawk; used to cut wood, hammer nails, start a fire with flint, and with its hollow head serving as a pipe.

Expedition members were carefully chosen for their skills: boatmen, blacksmiths, gunsmiths, foragers, hunters, and cooks. Both Lewis and Clark kept extensive journals and logs of weather, new plants and animals, geology, and topographic maps. They carried sextants, a portable map-making kit and surveying equipment, but many of their discoveries came through the help of local Indian tribes.

The explorers developed good relations with most of the tribes they met. They hired a 17-year-old Shoshone Indian woman named Sacagawea as an interpreter. She also gathered medicinal plants and food and shared her knowledge of living on the plains. The men learned to make pemmican from dried meat, berries, and fat pounded into cakes as "energy bars." Once, she rescued journals and medicines from a tipped canoe.

The Corps of Discovery continued west past the boundary of the Louisiana Purchase, climbed through Rocky Mountain passes, and journeyed down the Columbia River to the Pacific Ocean at the Oregon coast. After traveling 8,000 miles over 28 months, on September 23, 1806, the Corps of Discovery, having been given up for dead, once again docked in St. Louis, Missouri, to the cheers of 5,000 westerners. Lewis and Clark became enduring symbols of the new west.

BELOW *Aaron Burr fires the fatal bullet that cut down Alexander Hamilton and lodged next to his spine. The two men were both brilliant, but also flawed by their arrogance and ambition. Burr eventually died a ruined man.*

WEAPONS OF THE DUEL

AARON BURR

ALEXANDER HAMILTON

Though swords were as fashionable among eastern gentlemen as were knives down south (used in fights with the wrists tied together), pistols were the American duelist's most common weapon. One of the wronged parties would provide the single shot pistols, often in an elegantly boxed set. Seconds loaded the pistols with great care under strict observation. Shots were fired any time after the command to fire. Distances between duelists varied between 10 and 20 paces.

TROUBLE WITH BRITAIN —AGAIN

LEFT *The battle of Tippecanoe pitted an army of American troops against the Shawnee under Chief Tecumseh in 1811. The battle made a hero out of Indiana Territory Governor William Henry Harrison.*

By 1812, the United States had just over seven million people spread over 18 states and four large territories. In the salons of Europe, Americans were considered unlettered and vulgar. If the badly cooked food didn't kill you, the Red Indians would. Hygiene was spotty and the roads were mud tracks. From one state to another a traveler could hardly untangle English from the local idiom, and if the villages were rough, the growing cities were raw and uncouth, teeming with foul smells. But for all that, there were opportunities not available anywhere else. Multitudes from the British Isles and Europe crowded onto sailing vessels to seek their fortune in the United States.

One blemish on this Elysian state of affairs was the fact that the United States was still at war with Great Britain, 29 years after the Treaty of Paris had ended the Revolution. The British in Canada wanted to keep their forts around the Great Lakes. They encouraged the Indians to attack the settlers who were pouring into Kentucky, Ohio, and the Illinois Territory. At sea, American ships were turned away from trading with British colonies and had to slip into obscure ports to evade these trade laws. This trade friction had earlier been aggravated by the declaration of war between France and Britain in 1793. France was the principal trade partner of the United States and more than 250 American ships were confiscated by British warships for carrying contraband. For 10 years, American diplomats, spurred by an outraged public and government, sought redress, compromise, or anything to ease the situation. When Napoleon heated up the war again in 1802, Britain began to press

American sailors to fill the 150,000-man Royal Navy. "Once an Englishman, always an Englishman!" was the press-gang's cry.

President Jefferson wanted nothing to do with war. After fending off the war "hawks" in Congress for two terms, he headed home to Monticello, Virginia, and left the problems to James Madison, America's fourth president. Britain kept up pressure on the Indians throughout the frontier, and settlers were terrified. Finally, in November 1811, Indiana Territory Governor William Henry Harrison managed to pull together 900 American troops for a raid on a large village at Tippecanoe, which was commanded by Shawnee Chief Tecumseh's brother, the prophet Tenskwatawa. The American troops triumphed and, buoyed up by this victory, Congress urged Madison to give the British a final warning. The president fired off a demand for the elimination of trade restrictions on American ships. In truth, an American embargo on British trade

CHIEF TECUMSEH "CELESTIAL PANTHER"

Chief Tecumseh (1768–1813), whose name means "Celestial Panther Laying in Wait," became a full warrior at age 14 and later rose to become chief of his tribe. When asked to sell some of the Shawnee land, Tecumseh said: "Sell a country? Why not sell the air, the clouds, and the great sea, as well as the Earth? Did not the Great Spirit make them all for the use of his children?" He died in the Battle of the Thames on October 5, 1813.

was working. British merchants had realized they needed American trade, but the slow response of Parliament to Madison's ultimatum prompted a divided, partisan Congress to vote for war on Great Britain.

The United States was unprepared and had no plan and no strategy except the conquest of Canada. The American army was small, poorly trained, under-funded, and led by elderly generals out of touch with field command. The navy consisted of just 16 warships. Troops were rushed up toward American Fort Detroit to intimidate the British and Canadians into abandoning their ships and surrendering. But the unprepared army fell apart during the march and plans for their attack fell into British hands. The attack was a debacle. Next, in trying to evacuate Fort Dearborn before the Indians arrived, American Captain William Wells arrived late. He charged forward toward the swarm of Indians and, in a masterpiece of questionable judgment, began cursing the Indian chiefs. They shot him out of the saddle and ate his heart raw. So began the War of 1812.

LEFT *Napoleon Bonaparte crowned himself Emperor of France in 1804 and, helped by American dollars paid for Louisiana, he began the sack of Europe. Britain was dragged into war again, ending with Napoleon's final defeat at Waterloo (now in Belgium) on June 18, 1815.*

ABOVE *An engraving showing an eighteenth-century three-decker American warship surrounded by the tools of seamanship of the period, from navigation to examples of sailors' tools and nautical skills.*

ABOVE RIGHT *The British Royal Navy commanded the seas in the early nineteenth century as it continued to battle Napoleon Bonaparte. Its many ships needed crews and captains pressed sailors from American ships to serve in them.*

BELOW *A swivel gun, commonly used to threaten smaller ships or subdue any resistance, when loaded with grape shot. Marines usually manned the swivel guns in ship-to-ship confrontations.*

BRITISH SAILOR'S LIFE

Life in the Royal Navy was brutal. During war, press gangs roamed England dragging off farmers, laborers, drunks, and petty criminals to sea in exchange for "the King's shilling." Sailors learned by doing, spurred on with kicks and floggings for offenses. Food was fair at the start of a voyage and grew worse as scurvy wracked the crew after the fruit and vegetables were gone. Battle deaths and loss of limbs required frequent replacement crews. American sailors were frequent targets for the press gangs.

The Land War of 1812

LEFT *A contemporary view of the burned Washington Capitol buildings following the British attack in 1814. Considerable damage had been done to federal buildings including the White House, which was gutted by fire.*

BELOW *This view shows the east front of the President's House in Washington D.C. in 1807. The north and south porticos have been added. In 1814, British soldiers marched in and ate the dinner that had been prepared for President Madison.*

For the most part, the land battles in the poorly planned invasion of Canada constituted one American disaster after another. No sooner had Forts Detroit and Dearborn fallen than the public, Congress, and President Madison demanded new generals and victories. Tecumseh's attempt to unite the Indians now drew previously reluctant tribes—Creek, Delaware, Cherokee, and Kickapoos—to attack frontier settlers. Ambushes and massacres of families and whole communities enraged the public back east, who had been expecting quick victories up north.

William Henry Harrison, the hero of Tippecanoe, raised an army of keen-eyed woodsmen from Kentucky and Tennessee, and headed north to retake Fort Detroit. Patriotic zeal was dampened by torrential rains, swollen rivers, and impassable trails. He camped to wait for winter when frozen ground would be the Americans' ally. Meanwhile, British General Sir Isaac Brock with 1,600 troops and 300 Indians was seeking to defend against the crossing of the Niagara River by 6,000 American troops under General Stephen van Rensselaer. The inexperienced van Rensselaer divided his troops and on October 13 sent 800 troops across, having given orders for the rest of his army to cross downstream. This they failed to do and sat on the opposite bank while van Rensselaer's party under the command of Lieutenant Colonel Winfield Scott was shot up and captured. Unfortunately for the British, General Brock was killed, removing the best field commander they had.

Another attempt to ferry troops across the rushing Niagara River ended when 6,000 American infantry loaded into boats by General Alexander Smythe (who relieved Rensselaer), stopped in mid-stream and turned around. General Smythe retreated without explanation, calling off the expedition. He was quietly ousted from the army. Up at Lake Champlain, General Henry Dearborn's attack with 6,000

ABOVE *Ships of the British fleet are shown bombarding Washington and sailing up the Potomac River as troops are landed for the march inland. Government buildings were put to the torch on August 24, 1814.*

troops against Montreal on November 19, 1812, ran into trouble against the 1,900 British Canadian defenders. As the battlefield grew dark, the British troops withdrew, but the Americans pressed on. Dearborn's units became separated and soon began shooting at each other. Eventually, the general's army refused to go on and many of his troops packed up and went home because their enlistments had come to an end. Everywhere, what its critics called "Mr. Madison's War" was a disaster.

RIGHT *The map shows the many fronts on which the land war of 1812 was fought. While the U. S. Army sought to attack Canada and control the Great Lakes, the British Navy sacked Washington and shot up Fort McHenry in Baltimore, Maryland.*

By 1814, the British had prepared a three-pronged invasion, which would eventually target New York, Washington, Baltimore, and New Orleans in the deep south. Their orders from Admiral Alexander Cochrane were to burn, sack, and pillage as payback for American tactics in the north. After entering Chesapeake Bay on August 14, and driving off gunboat defenses, General Robert Ross marched his troops into the nation's capital and put the city to the torch. President Madison's wife, Dolley, barely got out of the residence before British troops arrived to find the evening dinner still warm on the table. They ate, and then burned the president's house down.

By September 11, the British fleet was arrayed against Baltimore's Fort McHenry. Kept at a distance by sunken blockade ships, the cannonade rained over 1,800 solid shot and shells into the fort. Rockets were fired to show gunners their targets. Standing at the rail of a ship in the harbor, Francis Scott Key scratched the lines of a poem that ended when he saw the American Star Spangled Banner still flying from the fort's rampart after the 25-hour bombardment.

Cochrane withdrew his ships. Up north, the New York-bound second prong of the British attack was blunted by American naval action on Lake Champlain against a British fleet. All that remained of the invasion plan was the thrust at New Orleans, a prize whose loss would make the Yankees squirm.

ABOVE RIGHT *Mrs. Rebecca Heald, wife of Fort Dearborn commandant Nathan Heald, defends herself during the 1812 massacre. She was shot six times and scalped. Her husband was shot through the hips. Both survived and were ransomed from the Indians.*

RIGHT *"Maddy in Full Flight": a contemporary British cartoon comment on President James Madison and the burning of Washington, D.C. in August 1814. Many Americans as well as British blamed the war on President Madison's bowing to war "hawks" in Congress.*

FRANCIS SCOTT KEY

A young Georgetown lawyer, Francis Scott Key (1779–1843) was asked to help free a close friend, Dr. William Beanes, who was being held on a British ship anchored off Baltimore in Chesapeake Bay. Key was rowed to the ship but not allowed to leave during the bombardment of Fort McHenry. From a distance of about eight miles, he watched the 25-hour bombardment of the fort. At its end, the American flag was still flying and Key wrote down his famous poem under the title, "The Defense of Fort McHenry."

THE WAR AT SEA & THE END OF THE BEGINNING

The large American frigate, *Constitution*, out-sailed the smaller British frigate, *Guerrière* captained by James Dacres, yet Dacres had demanded this showdown. The ships circled each other, maneuvering to gain the favorable wind, the gunner's advantage. Captain Isaac Hull, the *Constitution*'s skipper, held his fire. The Royal Navy had over 600 warships, 120 of which were 50–80 gun ships of the line—two- and three-deckers. The *Guerrière* was one of 116 fast frigates—the greyhounds of the fleet. Still, the American ship sailed inside her, holding closer to the wind. Dacres had challenged any of the inferior American navy ships to meet him. Though rated as a frigate, the *Constitution* was 50 feet longer, had a wider beam and mounted 50 iron guns, 24-pounders thrust through the gun deck ports and 32-pound carronades lined the upper deck. Gun captains squinted along their barrels.

"Now, boys! Pour it in to them!" screamed Hull as the *Guerrière* tried desperately to shear off. The 24-pounders fired as they bore, tearing up rigging, splintering wood, shattering taff rails, and blasting ratlines and hammock nettings to shreds. The 18-pound shot of the *Guerrière* bounced off the *Constitution*'s white oak strakes buttressed by live oak frames. With a tortured crack, the *Guerrière*'s mizzen mast

ABOVE *The frigate* Constitution, *(right) closes in on the* HMS Guerrière *to begin a historic duel. British balls bounced off "Old Ironsides" and the American ship dismasted her British opponent.*

U.S. FRIGATE CONSTITUTION

One of six frigates that made up the United States Navy at the start of the War of 1812, the Constitution was state-of-the-art at that time. Armed with 24-pound cannons and 32-pound carronades, she was a fighting ship. Constructed of 1,500 oak trees from Maine, the hull was sheathed in copper. All copper fittings were created by Paul Revere. She never lost a battle and was called "Old Ironsides" by her crew.

MAJOR GENERAL ANDREW JACKSON "OLD HICKORY"

A firebrand, Jackson (1767–1845) prospered in business and politics regardless of his short fuse and willingness to defend his "honor" against all comers. A man who had slandered his wife was killed by Jackson in a duel. He was the first resident of Tennessee to be elected to the House of Representatives and rose briefly to a seat in the Senate. Expecting the British to land troops near New Orleans, he used his personality, reputation, and old friendships to pull together a motley army that won the day. He was president from 1829 to 1837.

RIGHT *The Star Spangled Banner that flew over Fort McHenry is undergoing restoration at the Smithsonian Institution. The 32' x 42' flag sewn by Mary Pickersgill and her seamstresses was whittled away by souvenir hunters following the battle.*

LEFT *Master Commandant Oliver Hazard Perry transfers his colors from the sinking* Lawrence *to the* Niagara *during his victory over the British fleet in Lake Erie. He said, "We have met the enemy and he is ours."*

splintered, hung in the jumble of its ruined rigging, and then sagged over the side. Hull made his turn across the *Guerrière*'s bow, firing as he did so, and closed to 50 feet. The *Constitution*'s short carronades hammered their 32-pound balls into the tangle of up-ended guns, sprawled bodies, and fallen yard-arms.

Two hours after the contest began, *Guerrière* was holed to the waterline and dismasted. Dacres hauled down his colors and at 3:15 p.m., August 20, 1812, the British frigate *Guerrière* "… sank out of sight."

On land, the American army was being badly led into disaster after disaster, while at sea a new generation of brash young captains with their 38- and 50-gun frigates were winning battle after battle. British frigates *Frolic*, *Macedonian*, and *Java* all fell to American guns. On the Great Lakes, Oliver Hazard Perry built a fleet of gunboats and frigates. On September 10, 1813, after breaking a blockade by hand-hauling his ships across a sandbar, Perry sailed his Lake Erie fleet straight at the British. After a furious battle that saw Perry move his flag from a sinking wreck to another ship, the apparently victorious British fleet was stunned when he attacked yet again. Holed, raked, and sinking, the British ships surrendered.

The final act of the War of 1812 was played out on January 8, 1815, across a swampy Louisiana field. General Andrew Jackson looked down his lines behind redoubts made of cotton bales. His troops were creoles, Tennessee sharpshooters, free Blacks, local militia, Cajuns, and pirates. The British had been told these "dirty shirts" were cowards. With a roll of drums, the troops advanced on Jackson's position. An American cannon filled with scrap-iron ripped out and killed 200 at a stroke. Jackson's riflemen, four rows deep fired and fired and fired. Line after line of brave men fell. The drums pounded, rifles crashed, men died. The few surviving British soldiers were allowed to trudge back to their ships.

No one on that field knew that on Christmas Eve, 1814, American and British delegations had met in Ghent, Belgium, and signed a treaty ending the war. Neither country won. Both countries lost part of a generation of brave young men. Great Britain and the United States would never go to war again.

BELOW *A panoramic view of the Battle of New Orleans, as British troops hurl their lines against the trenches and cotton bales shielding General Andrew Jackson's forces. It was the last battle of the war.*

THE FOUNDING & THE FUTURE

The United States of America still had rough edges in 1815 as the country settled into picking over the recent conflict with Great Britain. Heroes were anointed and blame assigned, careers were shattered, and new faces became familiar. Everything seemed as fresh, raw, and unpainted as a new barn, smelling of wood sap, glue, and pine tar pitch. Government was still part of every conversation. Would it hold together? Could men elected by the people do the work of kings? They had made their choice these citizens of this new land who had roots in almost every country from which they could sail to its shores. How would this polyglot conglomeration sharing no single tradition, but partaking of the cacophony of a hundred traditions, manage to create a lasting culture and government?

They began slowly. The concept of being an "American" first and a Virginian, Pennsylvanian, North Carolinian, or New Yorker second was still a difficult fit, because local customs and local loyalties bound people together, regardless of what some papers and politicians might say. But they began slowly anyway. The United States was a nation of farmers, merchants, tradesmen, artisans, and men of letters

in science, philosophy, the healing arts, and clergy who came from all levels of society. But now, with their ground—twice won—beneath their feet, these Americans began to realize that, given the tools, they had the ability to rise to any level they sought

In 1815 it was the tools that were in short supply. Americans were forced to do business over long distances, they lacked the huge and complex infrastructure of roads, rivers, canals, bridges, and ports along 1,000 miles of seacoast. They relied on slaves for cheap farm labor. Their manufacturing capability was in its infancy and the merchant fleet was small by any standard. But this state of affairs

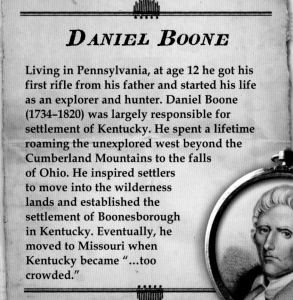

DANIEL BOONE

Living in Pennsylvania, at age 12 he got his first rifle from his father and started his life as an explorer and hunter. Daniel Boone (1734–1820) was largely responsible for settlement of Kentucky. He spent a lifetime roaming the unexplored west beyond the Cumberland Mountains to the falls of Ohio. He inspired settlers to move into the wilderness lands and established the settlement of Boonesborough in Kentucky. Eventually, he moved to Missouri when Kentucky became "...too crowded."

The Original "John Bull"

had been predictable. As Benjamin Franklin wrote in the *Pennsylvania Gazette* on August 24, 1749:

"In the settling of new countries, the first care of the planters must be to provide and secure the necessities of life; this engrosses their attention and affords them little time to think of anything farther … Agriculture and mechanical arts were of the most immediate importance; the culture of minds by the finer arts and sciences was necessarily postponed to times of more wealth and leisure."

That time was now upon Americans and they seized its significance. Eli Whitney's cotton gin, patented in 1794 (and with that patent upheld in 1807), automated the process of cleaning cotton and created a booming cash crop for the southern states. His American system of interchangeable parts for rifle manufacture sparked the idea of mass production and helped launch American industry. On August 10, 1807, Robert Fulton's steamboat *Clermont* chugged from New York City to Albany, taking 32 hours to travel 150 miles at an average speed of about 5 miles per hour. Twenty-six years later, the "John Bull" steam locomotive rolled down the rails of the Camden & Amboy Railroad—the first in New Jersey. That year, 1833, saw the first of America's fleet of clipper ships racing across the seas beneath clouds of sail. Immigrant wagons rutted trails to the west, crossed the Mississippi and followed the rivers into lands where Native Americans had roamed for generations.

The beneficiaries of the blood shed at Concord, Breed's Hill, Trenton, Valley Forge, Saratoga, Cowpens, and Yorktown prospered as the country grew and its people faced new challenges. The United States, with all its imperfections, had been founded and that work in progress still continues.

LEFT *Early steam locomotive, the "John Bull," was brought from England to Philadelphia and then to New Jersey to head one of the first American commercial railroad lines in the nineteenth century.*

RIGHT *This montage shows the dawning of new technology when America embraced the Morse code telegraph, the steam locomotive, and steamboat, as the nineteenth century opened up the future of the growing country.*

ELI WHITNEY

One of the great inventors of all time, Eli Whitney (1765–1825) personified the explosion of progress that came with the turn of the century and set the stage for the American industrial revolution. His cotton gin removed the seeds from cotton plants, allowing cotton to become a major southern cash crop. Later, he developed the concept of the assembly line when producing muskets for the army in 1798. His idea of creating interchangeable parts and sub-assemblies revolutionized manufacturing.

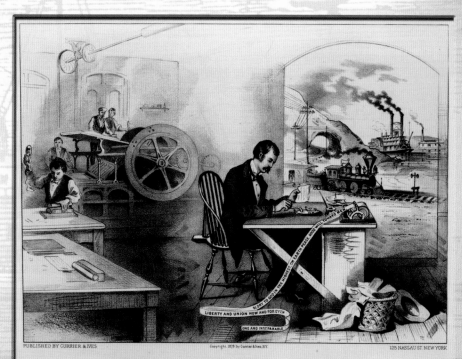

PUBLISHED BY CURRIER & IVES. Copyright 1876 by Currier & Ives, N.Y. 125 NASSAU ST. NEW YORK

THE PROGRESS OF THE CENTURY.
THE LIGHTNING STEAM PRESS. THE ELECTRIC TELEGRAPH. THE LOCOMOTIVE. THE STEAMBOAT.

INDEX